JORDAN

PROFILES • NATIONS OF THE CONTEMPORARY MIDDLE EAST
Bernard Reich and David E. Long, Series Editors

Jordan: Crossroads of Middle Eastern Events, Peter Gubser
South Yemen: A Marxist Republic of Arabia, Robert W. Stookey
Syria: Modern State in an Ancient Land, John Devlin
Turkey, George S. Harris
Iraq, Phebe Marr
Sudan, John Voll and Sarah Voll
United Arab Emirates, Malcolm Peck
North Yemen, Manfred W. Wenner
Lebanon, David C. Gordon

Also of Interest

The New Arab Social Order: A Study of the Social Impact of Oil Wealth, Saad Eddin Ibrahim
OPEC: Twenty Years and Beyond, edited by Ragaei W. El Mallakh
Economic Growth and Development in Jordan, Michael P. Mazur
The United Arab Emirates: Unity in Fragmentation, Ali Mohammed Khalifa
Libya: The Experience of Oil, J. A. Allan
Food, Development, and Politics in the Middle East, Marvin G. Weinbaum

JORDAN
Crossroads of
Middle Eastern Events

Peter Gubser

Westview Press • Boulder, Colorado

Croom Helm • London, England

093827

Profiles/Nations of the Contemporary Middle East

Photo credits: (A typical family scene) UNRWA photo by George Nehmeh; (Palestinian refugee children) UNRWA photo by Sue Herrick Cranmer; (An Amman vista) by Ann Barhoum; (Students) UNRWA photo by M. Nasr; (King Abdullah) by Janab Tutunji; all other photos courtesy of Jordan Information Bureau, Washington, D.C.

Jacket photo: A Roman forum in the ancient city of Jerash. Roman amphitheater in foreground. (Photo courtesy of the Jordan Information Bureau)

Copyright © 1983 by Westview Press, Inc.

Published in 1983 in the United States of America by
Westview Press, Inc.
5500 Central Avenue
Boulder, Colorado 80301
Frederick A. Praeger, President and Publisher

Published in 1983 in Great Britain by
Croom Helm Ltd.
Provident House
Burrell Row
Beckenham, Kent BR3 1AT

Library of Congress Catalog Card Number: 82-8361
ISBN (U.S.): 0-89158-986-4
ISBN (U.K.): 0-7099-1145-9

Printed and bound in the United States of America

For Annie

Contents

Tables and Illustrations

x TABLES AND ILLUSTRATIONS

Acknowledgments

My greatest debt is to the people of Jordan, who have been hospitable to me on many occasions and have provided considerable information on which this work is based. Although all those who helped cannot be cited, I wish to mention specifically Kamel Abu Jaber, Shaher Bak, Adnan Bakhit, Mohammed Barhoum, Albert Butross, Mazen Dajani, the people of Karak, Rami Khouri, Rose Marcos, Naif Mawla, Sulaiman Musa, Bassam Saket, Peter Salah, Rima and Janab Tutunji. Numerous Jordanian government officials were also helpful. Also in Jordan I enjoyed beneficial exchanges with Piero Bronzi, Carl Gotsch, Alan Hill, and Ralph Montee.

In the United States, I wish to extend my thanks to Cyril Bindah, Lucy Brown, and Alison Kelly of American Near East Refugee Aid (ANERA) for reading and commenting on the manuscript. Special gratitude goes to Ann Barhoum, Elizabeth Shine, and Daniel Sisken of ANERA for typing the manuscript, and to Dagny Svien for preparing the map. Others who have been of assistance on Jordanian topics are John Davis, Robert Fisher, Paul Jureidini, Ronald McClaurin, and the series editors, Bernard Reich and David Long. Shawki Barghouti, with whom I have discussed Jordanian issues in both Jordan and the United States, kindly read and made valuable comments on the manuscript.

To my wife, Annie, I extend warmest thanks for her many and wise observations on the work and her judicious help in editing it.

Naturally, I am solely responsible for the contents.

P.G.

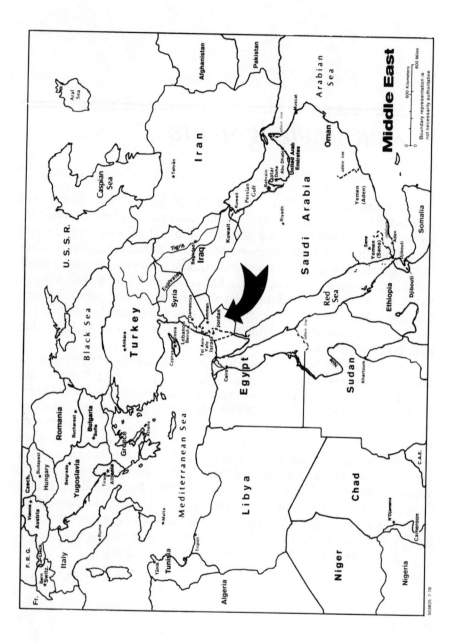

Middle East

1

Introduction

The Jordan of today is a unique consequence of a series of major, if not cataclysmic, historical events. It was born of World War I, as British, French, and Zionist forces divided up the Arab region of the crumbled Ottoman Empire. Lying east of the Jordan River on a Middle Eastern and world crossroads, the country was originally populated only sparsely by nomadic, seminomadic and settled peoples. The land area and population, however, were very significantly altered by the Arab-Israeli wars of 1948 and 1967. Following the 1948 war, Jordan annexed the West Bank, including East Jerusalem, and made citizens of its population as well as hundreds of thousands of other Palestinians from what has come to be known as pre-1967 Israel. The consequences of the 1967 war were even more traumatic: The West Bank was, and still is, as of this writing, subjected to Israeli military occupation, and about three hundred thousand Palestinians left the West for the East Bank, substantially adding to the population of this newly truncated land of few natural resources.

To this mixture of sweeping events must be added the Hashemite family, specifically Amir (Prince), later King, Abdullah, who was the founder of Jordan as a separate state, and his grandson, King Hussein, currently the world's longest-ruling head of state at the young age of forty-six. Despite the many vicissitudes they both experienced, these two Hashemite monarchs have exhibited a remarkable ability to stay in power and to rule their rapidly changing people – changing not only with respect to origin, but also in socioeconomic composition – as well as to survive the pressures and forces exerted from outside the kingdom, from the immediate Middle East and from the broader world. In order to retain power, both Abdullah and Hussein have relied on varying levels of repression and occasionally on their strong connections with Britain and the United States. Equally or more important has been the development of their personal legitimacy based on the Hashemites' leading role in the Arab nationalist movement; their family's claim of direct descendancy from the Prophet Muhammad and the religious feeling this relationship conveys; their regime's active pursuit of material development for their

1

people, whether they be indigenous Jordanians or Palestinians; and the perception of strength as well as simple longevity in the face of numerous challenges to the throne.

Within the context of its particular geographical position, history, and social makeup, Jordan faced and still faces a series of pressures unique among other developing countries. The sociopolitical division between the dominant East Jordanians and the refugee/immigrant Palestinians, who represent 55 percent or more of the combined population, results in a distinct tension, occasionally marked by harsh violence, such as occurred during the 1970 civil war. Another source of tension is the claim of Arab nationalism under various guises, such as the Arab Nationalist Movement, Ba'th party and "Nasserism," on the loyalty of Jordan's divided people as well as the constant political and ideological maneuvering of the Arab states. Directly related to the foregoing is the tension of sharing a long border with Israel, which necessitates high levels of expenditure on defense, absorbs considerable national energy, and continually puts Jordan in a front-line position.

Internally, Jordan, like many of its less developed cousins, has been attempting to develop economically and socially on a very sparse natural resource base, but with an artificially doubled population (and its normal population has a high fertility rate). Accordingly, most experts considered Jordan an economic basket case with no future, forever dependent on foreign aid and largess. However, despite ups and downs largely tied to wars and political crises, Jordan made moderate progress during the 1950s and 1960s, thanks partially to outside aid. By the middle to late 1970s, the country began experiencing a virtual boom, partly as a fallout from the phenomenal rise in petroleum prices enjoyed by its neighbors as well as from the Lebanese civil war (businesses and families with financial means moved to Jordan) and an efficient and judicious use of substantial foreign assistance. Ironically, for a country that suffered from a large surfeit of labor in the 1950s and 1960s, Jordan was in the late 1970s importing at any given time close to a hundred thousand unskilled and low-skilled laborers while it exported a larger number of its own skilled and highly educated workers.

Political development, though, is far behind economic and social development. King Hussein perhaps enjoys a certain legitimacy, and some informal means of political access and interaction exist, but processes and especially institutions for the people's political expression and participation are either very weak or nonexistent. As rapid social and economic progress proceeds apace, this disparity—and the internal perception of it—becomes more serious.

It is this interwoven complex of history, geography, and socioeconomic and political conditions that is to be investigated in this short work. Although the interrelationships and integrated nature of these various factors are emphasized, by necessity they are dealt with in a certain order. The environmental context is described in Chapter 2, and in the next chapter the nature of the people and their groupings are placed in this environmental setting. Chapter 4 describes the economy and Jordan's efforts at development. In Chapter 5, on Jordan's history, the pre–World War I period is only touched on, the emphasis being on the founding and growth of Jordan from 1920 to the contemporary period. Chapter 6, on politics and international relations, brings together all these topics in a political context and concludes the description and analysis.

A special note needs to be added on the West Bank. It will be dealt with as part of Jordan during that period when Jordan exercised control over the territory. During the other periods, before 1948 and after 1967, it will be brought into the discussion only as it relates to Jordan. In the post-1967 period, this relationship has remained particularly close: The people of the West Bank, including East Jerusalem, retain and enjoy the rights of their Jordanian citizenship; a number of "West Bankers" resident in the West Bank are still employees of the Jordanian government; the Jordanian government provides development funds for West Bank institutions; and so forth. No political statement about the future of the West Bank is made or intended by the different treatments of the East and West Banks in the post-1967 period. Rather, as with the official Jordanian statistics for the same period, practicality and reality restrict the discussion to the East Bank rather than the whole of 1948–1967 Jordan.

2

Environment

Almost a landlocked country, Jordan is bordered on the west by Israel, the north by Syria, the east by Iraq, and the east and south by Saudi Arabia. Jordan also enjoys a 16-mile (26-kilometer) coastline on the Red Sea, the focus of which is the port of Aqaba. As to size, the East Bank is about 35,000 square miles (90,649 square kilometers). The West Bank, which is bounded on the north, west and south by Israel and separated from the East Bank by the Jordan River and Dead Sea, covers about 2,100 square miles (5,440 square kilometers).

Very much reflective of Jordan's history, these borders have not been stable during its short existence as a separate state; they have gone through four de jure or de facto changes. Namely, the original borders of the amirate (princedom) as established in 1920–1922 did not extend to Aqaba and Iraq to the south and east respectively and did not include the West Bank. The acquisition of Aqaba and territorial extensions to Iraq were settled in 1924–1925, after a series of claims, counterclaims, moves, and negotiations involving the British (mandatory power), Amir Abdullah, Sharif Hussein of Mecca, King Ali of Hijaz (the latter two being respectively the father and brother of Amir Abdullah), and the Saudis, who conquered the Hijaz, including Mecca and Jidda, in 1924–1925. By the early 1930s, these new borders were essentially recognized as legitimate by both Abdullah's Transjordan and Ibn Saud's Saudi Arabia. In 1965, Jordan and Saudi Arabia officially exchanged land, giving the former a longer coastline at Aqaba and the latter added desert territory to the east, although any potential mineral exploitation in the traded territories is to be shared.

The other Jordanian border changes are central to the underlying Arab-Israeli dispute, namely the gain and loss of the West Bank. In 1948, Jordan's Arab Legion occupied the West Bank during the fighting with the newly founded Israeli state. Following the desire of King Abdullah and at the request of some Palestinian notables, the territory was officially annexed to Jordan in 1950. In the 1967 Arab-Israeli war, Jordan lost the West Bank to Israeli military occupation. The de facto border is

6

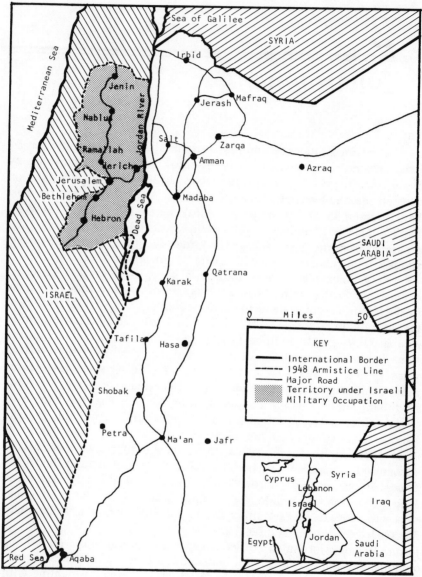

Jordan.

now at the Jordan River. However, Jordan has not relinquished sovereignty, and it maintains an official relationship with its citizens in the West Bank, including East Jerusalem.

Jordan's terrain and weather are marked by stark contrasts. The most striking feature, perhaps, is the Dead Sea, the lowest point on earth at 1,296 feet (395 meters) below sea level. To the north of this sea is the Jordan Valley, which is rapidly being developed for agricultural purposes by the construction of a sophisticated irrigation network. This very low area also extends to the south of the Dead Sea and is currently being studied for its development potential. The entire giant rift is bordered by precipitous hills that in a very short distance drop from an average of 3,500 feet (1,067 meters) above sea level to the Jordan Valley and Dead Sea. Beyond these hills is the central highland region of Jordan, which stretches from north of Ma'an to the Syrian border, widening slightly like a wedge as one moves north. Its terrain varies from extensive, slightly sloped plains to abrupt hills too steep to cultivate. In addition, the region is occasionally cut deeply by wadis (valleys), making transportation difficult and forcing the main north-south road and railway eastward into the desert. South of Ma'an, the land is more mountainous, dropping down to sea level at Aqaba. To the east lies the Syrian (or North Arabian) Desert, only occasionally broken by oases or catchments where cultivation is possible.

Soil types vary with the terrain. In the Jordan Valley, except in areas marked by highly saline soil, the land is quite fertile when provided with irrigation water. On the central plateau the soils are in some places light and shallow, suitable only for grains, and in others deep and suitable for fruit growing. The more hilly areas are subject to an ambitious reforestation program, the results of which are quite visible in selected parts of Jordan. To the east of the plateau, where only marginal cultivation but considerable animal husbandry is possible, are found three distinct kinds of desert: basalt from volcanic lava, flintstone, and the classic silicon sand. These three meet, unique to the world, at the Azraq oasis, 50 miles (80 kilometers) east of Amman.

Like the terrain, rainfall varies considerably in this small country, from more than 25 inches (640 millimeters) annually to virtually nil. The Jordan Valley receives from 2 to 8 inches (50 to 200 millimeters), which obviously renders the region infertile without irrigation. The northern part of the central plateau wedge enjoys averages of up to 25 inches (640 millimeters); in the southern part the average falls to 12 to 14 inches (300 to 360 millimeters), which is just adequate for grains such as wheat and barley. To the east and south of the plateau, the rainfall declines to virtually none. Typical of the Mediterranean climate, it rains only during

A shepherd tending his flock.

the period from mid-fall to mid-spring. Rainfall is erratic as well as low. For example, in a plateau region such as Karak, which averages 15 inches (380 millimeters), yearly precipitation may vary from 8 to 25 inches (200 to 640 millimeters), making farming a true exercise in planning in uncertainty.

Temperatures in the Jordan Valley are mild to hot, never cold, and the plateau and desert enjoy mild summers, with a few hot days, and moderate winters, with the temperature often dropping below freezing and occasional snow.

Jordan, unlike many of its sister Arab countries, has not discovered exploitable petroleum reserves. Despite exploration over the decades by many companies of various nationalities, liquid petroleum has not been found. Oil shale, however, is available in quantity in widely dispersed areas. Jordan is investigating ways to exploit this shale, but as long as the technologies require considerable water, they will have only limited applicability, if that, in Jordan.

Extractive industries have been built or are being built on the basis of other recoverable minerals. The most highly developed is phosphates, located in Rusaifa, Hasa, and Shidiya. This mineral, which is used as a fertilizer, has been mined since the 1930s, but in the 1960s Jordan embarked on a major program to exploit it in much greater quantity and using more sophisticated means. Potash is abundant in the Dead Sea and is now extracted by Israel from its portion of the sea. Jordan will start production from its side in the early 1980s in the single most expensive industrial project in the country's history.

Jordan also contains limited, but known, quantities of certain ores, such as copper, manganese, and iron. These are not currently exploited. Other minerals, such as gypsum for the cement industry and kaolinite for ceramics, however, are being extracted, albeit in limited quantities.

In sum, Jordan is poor in natural resources: soil, rainfall, and minerals. In contrast, it is rich in human resources, to which we turn in the next chapter.

3

People

It is typical of the nature of Jordan that it is difficult to count the population. In the November 1979 census, it was decided that only individuals residing in the East Bank and those absent from the East Bank for one year or less would be counted. Using these rules, the census came up with 2,152,273 Jordanians. In this count, though, two distinct groups are not included. The first was West Bankers (including pre-1967 East Jerusalemites), although these people retain Jordanian citizenship, have Jordanian passports, and enjoy other national rights; their total was approximately 850,000. The second was the hundreds of thousands of Jordanian citizens, a majority of whom are Palestinian, who live outside Jordan and have done so for more than a year. These are people residing mostly in Kuwait, Saudi Arabia, United Arab Emirates, and other oil-rich countries; others are scattered around the Arab world, Europe, and the United States. These groups were excluded to establish the true in-country population for planning purposes and to avoid the obvious difficulty of conducting a census in territory occupied by the Israeli military as well as certain problems, including political identification, in counting Jordanians resident abroad.

The natural growth rate, as figured by the Jordanian Statistics Bureau, was 3.4 percent, a high rate by world standards, but certainly matched by some other developing countries. The growth rate had actually increased from the 3.1 percent rate that prevailed in the 1960s and from the even lower rate in previous decades due to the broad improvement of health conditions.

The natural growth rate, however, by no means accounts for the present Jordanian population, not even half of it. To observe this, it is necessary to follow the various population estimates and counts throughout Jordan's brief history. As only two censuses[1] have been undertaken in Jordan, in 1961 and 1979, and major population shifts have resulted from warfare in the region, many of the figures, albeit useful, are subject to doubt.

11

The earliest East Jordan population figures are based on estimates by tribal shaykhs (chiefs) and village leaders. Thus, in 1922, just as Amir Abdullah was consolidating his hold on the territory, it was thought that 122,430 lived in villages and 102,950 were nonvillage tribespeople, for a total of 225,380. By the late 1930s, the estimate, this time by the provincial governors, had grown to 300,214, including 31,500 who were added when the southern border was extended past Ma'an to Aqaba. By 1946, however, the estimate on the basis of identity cards was 433,659, of whom 334,398 were in villages and towns and 99,261 were nonsettled bedouin.[2] The 1946 estimate is considered to be the most accurate of the above and indicates that the earlier figures were probably considerably underestimated.

The 1948–1949 Arab-Israeli war radically changed this population picture, more radically than it did the territorial makeup of Jordan. To the modest population of four hundred thousand plus souls were rapidly added about four hundred thousand Palestinians who were residents of and remained on the West Bank and around four hundred fifty thousand Palestinian refugees who had fled the newly founded Israeli state. In addition, tens of thousands of Palestinians not classified as refugees and thus unable to benefit from the United Nations refugee relief program fled to both the West and East banks of Jordan. About one-quarter of the refugees originally came to the East Bank, the balance settling in the West Bank. During the subsequent years, the Palestinian population continued to move to the East Bank, and particularly to the capital, Amman, yet no figures on the annual flow are available.[3]

The next big population shift occurred with the June 1967 Arab-Israeli war and the loss of the West Bank to Israeli military occupation. Again numbers are not totally accurate, but from data from the United Nations Relief and Works Agency for Palestine Refugees (UNRWA), Jordan, and Israel, it may be estimated that two hundred sixty-five thousand came to the East Bank from the West Bank and another forty-five thousand came from the Gaza Strip. The majority were official refugees and quickly settled in emergency camps, but many others poured into Amman and other cities, such as Irbid and Salt. From 1968, the flow from the West Bank to the East Bank (and often on to the Arabian, or Persian, Gulf) continued at a rate varying from two to three thousand to up to the 1981 level of more than twenty thousand per year.[4]

In broad strokes, the effect of these radical population and territorial adjustments was to treble the population in 1948 by the inclusion of a sizable number of refugees as well as the West Bank indigenous population. Correspondingly, the population shifted from one characterized by a vast majority of East Jordanians to one with a strong majority of Palestinians. No longer was Jordan a small, overlooked amirate; it had become instead a small kingdom central to the Arab-Israeli controversy. The 1967 war lost the West Bank to Israeli occupation (albeit Amman has not disclaimed sovereignty), but it added considerable Palestinian population to the East Bank. And most observers now consider the East Bank to have a Palestinian majority. This tumultuous pattern indicates the real human scope and consequences of recent Middle Eastern history.

The final aspect of population ebb and flow to be mentioned is the out- and in-migration for labor purposes. The actual number of Jordanians working and living, for short or long terms, outside Jordan is not precisely known. Estimates for 1980–1981 by Jordanian officials usually put the number at around five hundred thousand, of whom a hundred fifty to two hundred thousand are in the labor force – that is, fully 30–35 percent of the Jordanian labor force. In 1968, in contrast, it is estimated that only 5 percent of the labor force was outside Jordan. This movement of workers, and, among the upper-level group, of their families as well, is a phenomenon resulting directly from the boom in the oil-rich countries, especially around the Arabian Gulf. On the one hand, this labor shift has greatly disrupted certain Jordanian economic sectors and depleted human resources trained at Jordanian expense. On the other hand, it has contributed quite valuable remittances to the economy, and the presence of large numbers of Jordanian nationals, although many are Palestinians, in states with small populations gives Jordan a certain influence in these countries.

In 1980 it was reliably estimated that there were eighty to one hundred thousand foreign workers in Jordan, half of whom were Egyptian. They were mostly unskilled or semiskilled laborers and for the most part were not accompanied by their families. The irony of this labor importation is that in the 1960s and before Jordan had a major labor surplus, which was largely a result of the artificial population increase stemming from the influx of the Palestinian refugees. In the later 1950s, Jordanian and expatriate economists were estimating that one-quarter of the work force was unemployed and that there was a high rate of underemployment among those working, especially those in agriculture.

As is to be expected, the population is largely concentrated in the high rainfall belt, namely the northwest corner of the country. The density diminishes as one moves south through Madaba, Karak, and Tafila. On the desert margins, around water sources, are scattered villages, mostly of settled bedouin, as well as the black tents of the nomadic bedouin. Breaking the pattern of population concentration in relatively high rainfall regions are the eighty thousand residents of the Jordan Valley, who live there because of the recently developed irrigation system. (People have long lived in this great depression, but in smaller numbers and living off a more marginal economy.) Two other unusual aspects of the residential pattern need to be mentioned. First, the official refugee population in 1980 was 716,000, or one-third of the country's population; a little more than two hundred thousand, or 10 percent of the country's population, are in rural and urban-based UNRWA camps, located in the northwest of the country along with the bulk of the population.[5] The balance live in urban areas, largely Amman, and a few are found in the villages. Second, although the attraction of urban areas is common in developing regions, Jordan, as a consequence of its unique history and the refugee influx, is a special case, with more than half the population concentrated in the five largest cities and towns. In 1980 Amman itself had 30 percent of the country's population, and if one counts the entire metropolitan area, including Zarqa, the figure reaches nearly 50 percent. It is usually estimated that the city's population is 75 percent Palestinian.

Material on age distribution and the labor force must be calculated from the 1961 census and household surveys of the early 1970s because the Jordanian Statistics Bureau had not yet fully tabulated, analyzed, and published the 1979 census material as of this writing. According to these data, the group from 0 to 14 years is 46.5 percent of the population; the working-age group, from 15 to 64 years, is 50.6 percent; and the group 65-years and older constitutes 2.8 percent. The actual labor force is about four hundred thirty thousand, or 20 percent of the population, which indicates a 1 : 4 dependency ratio. These data indicate that Jordan has one of the youngest populations and highest dependency ratios in the world. The causes of this are, most probably, the high birth rate and the emigration of the work force to the Arabian Gulf. Ironically, labor emigration did not greatly change the size of the labor force and the dependency ratio because previously the chronically unemployed had dropped out of the labor force, lowering its numbers about the same amount as emigration did in the 1970s.

NATIONAL AND MINORITY GROUPS

Jordan is sharply divided by a series of partially overlapping groupings of a mixed national, cultural, social, and economic nature. The national and cultural differentiations, the subject of this section, are most vividly represented by the Palestinian Jordanians (as distinguished from, for want of a better term, the East Jordanians, that is Jordanians whose families originally came from the East Bank of the Jordan River) as well as, to a lesser extent, by groups based on distinctions between Muslims and Christians and ethnic distinctions between Arabs and non-Arabs (Circassians, Shishanis, Armenians). The subsequent section takes up another set of groups based on lifestyle and type of residential pattern, namely nomadic bedouin, villagers, refugees of the camps, and urban dwellers, in addition to the socioeconomic divisions, which are most starkly found in the urban areas.

Palestinians

The distinction between the Palestinians and the East Jordanians constitutes the most serious and, at times, nation-threatening cleavage in Jordan – and it is of relatively recent origin. Prior to the 1948 Arab-Israeli war, there were solely East Jordanians in the amirate of Jordan. One of the major consequences of this war, however, was the incorporation of the West Bank into Jordan and the granting of citizenship to all residents of the West Bank as well as to the Palestinian refugees who found themselves in the East and West banks after the war. Although not all Palestinians can be characterized in this manner, it may be said that a high proportion of the Palestinian Jordanians have fundamentally different national aims from those of the East Jordanians. The latter focus on the East Bank and wish to see its economic and social development; regaining the West Bank or even all of Palestine is perhaps desired but is not very high on their priority list. On the other hand, the Palestinians' primary national aim is to regain part or all of Palestine; this is especially true for those in the camps and those who came to Jordan during or after the 1967 war. These Palestinians fundamentally see Jordanian citizenship as a convenience rather than an identity or a loyalty.

In addition, cultural, educational, and social differences existed that divided the two groups in the early years[6] and that have left a legacy thirty years later. East Jordan of 1948 was predominantly rural. The people lived in villages or bedouin tents; a few small towns, such as Irbid, Salt, Amman, and Karak existed, but they had only five to thirty thousand people and very few urban characteristics. In contrast, Palestine had a decidedly urban sector, with concentrations in port cities and towns such as Haifa, Jaffa, and Gaza and in the principal inland towns of Jerusalem, Hebron, Nablus, and Nazareth. Compared to the towns of East Jordan, these cities were much more substantial, ranging from twenty-five thousand to sixty-five thousand. This relative urbanization was reflected in other sectors. Daniel Lerner, in his seminal book *The Passing of Traditional Society*, pointed out that, comparing the West and East Banks, 50 percent of West Bank Palestinian children attended school while 20 percent of the East Bank children did.[7] Similarly, Palestinians had proportionately three times as many doctors, and East Jordanians suffered from an infant mortality rate 50 percent higher than that of the Palestinians.

In a social sense, these gross data translated into a Palestinian feeling of superiority over their East Jordanian neighbors. They believed that they possessed superior knowledge, skills, and culture, and they resented the East Jordanian political dominance. Many Palestinians used these skills, capital, and energies to rebuild quickly their lives. One of the consequences of this was the phenomenal growth of Amman and its development as a Palestinian town, even though it is the capital of Jordan. Others, however, languished in the refugee camps or in unemployment in the squalid poorer sections of Amman and other towns. It should be noted that a significant portion of these sociocultural differences disappeared by the late 1970s due to development efforts in Jordan. To varying degrees, though, their legacy and the separate identities of Palestinians and East Jordanians do persist.

Despite these contrasts, many mutual ties and relationships existed. One example is the traditional family links between Nablus and Salt and between Hebron and Karak. These ties involved frequent contact, marriages, and trade. In addition, East Jordanians were consumers of Palestinian publications (as well as publications from Damascus and Egypt) and radio broadcasts (the country had no radio station prior to 1948). On a broader level, the two groups are part of the same Arab culture, speak a very similar dialect of Arabic, and for the most part adhere to Sunni Islam. Finally, although the Ottoman provincial lines were never entirely clear and changed with some rapidity, the two areas were always part of the greater Syria region of the Ottoman Empire and at times were ruled, at least partially, by the same Ottoman governor. Following World War I, the relationship of Transjordan (East Jordan) to Britain's Palestine mandate was not entirely clear, partially because one of Sharif Hussein's sons, Amir Faisal, was attempting to establish an Arab kingdom that was to include Transjordan. With the failure of Faisal's efforts in 1920, Britain asserted control, but it was not clear if Transjordan fell under the terms of the Balfour Declaration. This question was made academic in 1922 when Britain legally distinguished Transjordan from Palestine, an action that was internationally accepted. After this date, the Palestinians and East Jordanians started to develop separately in an administrative sense.

The evolution of the Palestinians in Jordan to 1980 has created distinct internal divisions with respect to their perception of and relationship to Jordan. Those families that came to reside in Jordan prior to 1948 identify themselves as Jordanians. For the most part, they prospered commercially, professionally, and in government service. A second group is the 1948 refugees, whether officially registered with the UNRWA or not, who do not live in the camps. This group, to use a popular term, is the silent majority. It has enjoyed considerable success commercially and in the professions; some of its members are in the

A typical family scene in the old quarter of East Jerusalem.

bureaucracy, and a few have achieved positions of significant responsi-
bility and authority. Although almost all would profess to want to regain
the West Bank and/or Palestine and to return there, most have invest-
ments in the East Bank in homes and business. To uproot themselves
voluntarily for an uncertain future in a fledgling West Bank state or entity would certainly be problematic for them.

A third group is the noncamp residents who came in 1967. They
maintain a stronger loyalty to the West Bank and to Palestine and may be
characterized as somewhat more militant and closer to the refugees in
the camps. Many have not yet achieved the economic success of the 1948
refugees, but like the 1948 group they would be jeopardizing jobs and
perhaps property if they decided to return. The fourth group is the
refugees, from both 1948 and 1967, who still live in the camps. Disgruntled, unsettled, despondent, militant or potentially so – these are the
words used to describe these long-term residents of the camps, in which
a whole generation has been born, brought up, and is now starting to
bring up a second generation. These also are the people most dependent
on the UNRWA for housing, rations, schooling, health, and welfare services. (The poor of the other groups are also dependent on the UNRWA
for all but housing and perhaps rations.) Although today most of the

camp refugees are employed, this was not the case prior to 1973, when unemployment was the norm.

Despite these differences, with the exception of the first and smallest group, the vast majority identify themselves as Palestinians and have a fundamental attachment to the hills of the West Bank or the plains of Haifa and Jaffa. Some, perhaps most, are willing to drop the claim on the latter for possession of the former, whether they wish to move there or not.

King Hussein's position with respect to these questions has remained clear and consistent since the mid-1970s. After the 1974 Arab Summit Conference in Rabat, he and all Arab states recognized the Palestine Liberation Organization (PLO) as the sole legitimate representative of the Palestinian people. He has not, however, dropped Jordan's claim of sovereignty over the West Bank, including East Jerusalem. As to the future relationship of the West Bank to Amman, this question is officially left open, theoretically making anything from complete union, to loose federation, to independent statehood possible. In taking this position, the Amman government continually says that the Palestinians of the West Bank (and the Gaza Strip, although Jordan has no residual sovereignty claims there) have the right of self-determination, which would allow for any of these alternatives.

Religious and Ethnic Minorities

Officially no minorities exist in Jordan. Thus, in a 1951 Jordanian government notice to the United Nations Educational, Scientific and Cultural Organization (UNESCO), it was stated that "there are no minorities in the Hashemite Kingdom of Jordan, and all Jordanians, whatever the differences in origin, religion, or language, are equal before the law."[8] This concept was reaffirmed in the Jordanian constitution promulgated on January 8, 1952, in which the basic rights of freedom and equality before the law are recognized for all citizens, regardless of race or religion. As in most countries, such an official position is an ideal, but in Jordan it is one that is not abused by the government on any consistent basis and generally not by the society either. Actually, in some spheres, most minorities proportionately enjoy more benefits than the rest of the population. Despite the government's 1951 statement, however, minorities in the accepted sense of the word do exist.

Christians form an ancient community in Jordan, dating back to the period shortly after the dawn of Christianity. In the East Bank, they are found in significant numbers in the town of Karak and its surrounding villages and in Madaba, Salt, and Amman. In the West Bank, they live in Jerusalem, Ramallah, and Bethlehem and in some of the villages surrounding each of the three towns. Their numbers, as with figures for the

An ancient Byzantine map of Jerusalem found in a Madaba church.

rest of Jordan, are not well established. Most recent estimates put the
Christian population at one hundred twenty-five thousand in the East
Bank,[9] of which a little less than two thirds are Greek Orthodox, about a
third Greek Catholic, and the balance Roman Catholic and a few hundred Protestants, Armenians, Assyrians (Nestorians), and Syrian Orthodox (Jacobites). The latter three groups are not ethnically Arab, but the
great majority speak Arabic as well as another mother tongue, or Arabic
only.

The largest group of Christians, the Greek Orthodox, fall under the
authority of the Greek Orthodox patriarch of Jerusalem, who is the
highest religious leader for the Greek Orthodox of Jordan, the West
Bank, and Israel. The church's liturgy is in Greek and Arabic; its top officials are largely of Greek origin while the balance of the clergy is Arab.
The Greek Catholics split off from the Greek Orthodox church to form a
Uniate church in 1709, but many of this group in the East Bank did not
convert until late in the nineteenth century. The patriarch of this church
has authority over the region stretching from Alexandria to Jerusalem to
Antioch but is obedient to the pope in Rome. The clergy is Arab, as is the
liturgy. The other Christians came to the area because of the attractions
of Jerusalem and in search of economic opportunity. The Protestants are

the exception. They are a product of European and U.S. missionary conversion efforts in the late nineteenth and early twentieth centuries. Virtually all converts are from the other Christian sects, not from the Muslim community. Finally, it should be noted that a number of Palestinian Christians are found on the East Bank; they identify with their fellow Muslim Palestinians. The East Jordanian Christians, on the other hand, identify strongly with Jordan.

The internal organization of the East Bank Christians has two aspects, one of which is unique in the Middle East. First, the churches form a framework, admittedly divided, for Christian organization and communal activity. Following long Middle Eastern tradition and somewhat related to the old Ottoman *millet* (community) system, each sect has courts that are responsible for personal status law, which involves questions of marriage, divorce, inheritance, the treatment of orphans, and the like. In matters affecting the group as a whole the ecclesiastical leaders may speak for the community. Second, and this is singular among Middle Eastern Christians, the Christians of Karak, Madaba, and Salt are organized along tribal lines very similar to those of their Muslim brothers. (See the following section for a description of the tribal system.) The combination of the tribal system with the highly structured and organized nature of the church, in contrast to the simpler organization of the mosque, gives the Christians a greater group cohesiveness than the Muslims. This is especially true because their very status as a minority with a strong identity tends to pull them together.

With respect to education, Christian missionaries, Roman Catholic and Protestant, set up schools in the 1870s and 1880s in Karak, Madaba, and Salt and expanded them to other areas during the following decades. Although Muslims were and are welcome to attend the schools, Christians have definitely benefited more from them, attaining a higher educational standard than their Muslim counterparts. (With the expansion of state education since the 1950s, this gap is now narrowing.) Partly as a consequence of education, but also of cultural differences from traditional Muslims, Christians more readily entered commerce in the early days. The legacy of this history is that Christians are disproportionately represented in business, banking, and the like. Their technical expertise and loyalty to the kingdom have also allowed many to advance to responsible official positions. For example, the current heads of the National Planning Council and the Royal Scientific Society, both crucial for Jordan's important development efforts, are Christian. Each cabinet has had one to three Christians, albeit it is recognized that a Christian will not serve as prime minister. Also, parliament traditionally has proportional or slightly more than proportional Christian representation based on a district-communal distribution system.

Relations between Christians and Muslims have generally been cordial and close. Social visiting is quite common, as is participation in each other's religious ceremonies. In previous generations many Muslims had their children baptized, and a few Christians took more than one wife. Even today, a village Christian in Karak district with a barren wife may take a second without divorcing the first. Very rarely, though, do marriages occur across religious lines. Finally, the people continually express their mutual tolerance for one another and are quite proud of their good relations as compared with those in the rest of the Middle East.[10]

Differences and minor strains do, however, exist. Like many minorities with relatively high levels of education, the Christians sometimes feel superior to their Muslim countrymen. Likewise, they occasionally complain that not all positions in the government are open to them. On an official level, even though the Jordanian constitution recognizes freedom and equality for all, it also recognizes Islam as Jordan's official religion. Stemming from this and from pressure by certain Muslim groups, a Public Education Law was passed in 1955 (it was dropped and not reintroduced and enforced until 1966) that essentially brought curricula of all private – mostly Christian – schools into conformity with the state schools. This law was strongly opposed by the Christian communities, but nationalist Muslims eventually prevailed. Since the late 1970s, the Middle East has witnessed a period of Islamic fervor. This phenomenon has caused certain Muslim practices to be emphasized broadly in Jordan, and some Christians express concern over this trend.

The only significant ethnic minorities in Jordan are the Circassians and their Shishani cousins, who number twenty-five thousand and two thousand respectively. These groups speak different Caucasian languages, but they are both Muslim (although the former are Sunni, like the balance of Jordanian Muslims, and the latter adhere to the Shiʿa sect). They moved from Caucasia to the southern part of the Ottoman Empire in the 1880s following the 1878 Congress of Berlin, which, inter alia, formally ceded Caucasian territory to Russia. At that time the Ottomans were attempting to secure greater control over their empire, and they thus encouraged the Circassians to settle in the northern part of what was to become East Jordan (and in southern Syria as well), where they assisted the empire in keeping communication lines open and provided a counterbalance to the bedouin.

Today, the Circassians and Shishanis are not politically assertive as a group. Nevertheless, due to their loyalty to the Hashemites, and most probably to their minority status, they enjoy a disproportionately high number of positions in the government, military, and security forces.

Despite their small number, they have two seats in parliament, of which traditionally one is held by a Circassian and the other by a Shishani. Many have served in cabinets, and one Circassian notable, Saᶜid al-Mufti, was prime minister. Most Circassians are farmers, businessmen, and landlords. Virtually all speak Arabic, and numerous marriages are now being contracted between the Circassians and the Arab Muslim majority group.

LIVING PATTERNS

In this section, the subject is divided into several subparts. The first addresses common kinship and tribal characteristics applicable to Jordanian society. The second divides the population according to the various relevant residential groups, and the last describes briefly the pattern of socioeconomic stratification.

Kinship and Tribal Systems

The Jordanians, like most Arabs, reckon kinship through the male line. Politically and socially this patrilineal pattern is significant, for it tends to create neat, segregated units and subunits within a larger group. Also, a man's identity is more strongly attached to these smaller units than any other group, for the behavior of an individual is considered to be the extension of that of his kin, and conversely, the actions of a man's blood relatives heavily reflect upon him. In addition, it is usual in Arab-Jordanian society for all individuals with the same family name (often including members in several villages) to consider themselves descendants in the male line of one man in the remote past. In almost all cases, however, the lineage of four or five generations is the only true descent line, and more important, this kin group is usually the largest that can take joint action as a kin group.

The kin unit is further marked by the marriage preference for one's parallel cousin (father's brother's daughter). In traditional Arab law, an unmarried man has the legal right to marry his closest parallel cousin; and not until he has given his permission may she marry another. If no first cousin on the paternal side is available, two other preferences become operative. Paternal cousins of a lesser degree are frequently chosen, and a cross-cousin (mother's brother's daughter or father's sister's daughter) may also be sought. Quite often, because of the general marriage pattern, a cross-cousin is a paternal cousin as well, only of a more distant relationship. This marriage pattern, then, creates a web of both kin and conjugal ties within a relatively small unit, binding its members together and giving it some features of a bilateral kin system. The incidence of parallel-cousin marriage is not statistically known for Jordan, but studies of various Arab villages indicate that 10 to 15 percent are of this type. Apparently, this percentage approaches the maximum possible, given the demographic limit on the availability of parallel cousins. Marriages within the larger lineage may constitute 30 to 70 percent of all a village's marriages.

As a consequence of both the patrilineal and marriage patterns, all the descendants in the male line of a man who lived four or five generations ago may be considered as a corporate group with a common identity and some common sociopolitical functions. Very often there will be one spokesman or leader for this kin group reinforced by marriage ties, and he will deal with the higher-level leaders in the village, tribe, town, or government.

For the most part, these lineages tend to be located in one residential area, neighborhood, encampment, or village (often just one part of a village, in a clan barrio fashion) or at most in a few neighboring villages. This is because the traditional occupations – agriculture, local industry, and crafts – tie individuals and families to a given area. However, a new pattern is beginning to emerge among the educated, the skilled, and even the common laborers who move to other areas to seek employment. Their lineages have changed from residential units to functionally extended families, usually smaller than a lineage but still maintaining extensive and intense contact and cooperation. Marriages in these functionally extended families tend to be contracted with individuals outside the kin group because the young people and their families are seeking spouses who are educated like themselves and who bring more to their families in a social and, ultimately, political sense.

For the more traditional Jordanians, marriage preferences are endogamous according to kin group, tribal section and tribe, village, region, and religion. There are two primary reasons for kin endogamy: to keep property within the family and to reinforce the larger kin group as a political group. Allowing and contracting marriages outside the family, but in the village or the near vicinity, also has strong social and political implications. On the one hand, it can create a link with another lineage, which may help solidify an already tenuous tie, strengthening both groups with additional numbers. On the other hand, marriage ties are often used for communication between estranged groups: A woman has the right to visit her family, or a brother has the right to visit his sister.

Marriage and divorce are regulated by religious law. Multiple marriages, although allowed for Muslims, are not very common. Divorce is permitted for Muslims and to a lesser degree for Greek Orthodox, but neither group practices it widely. For Muslims, aside from ordinary social and family pressures not to divorce, there is a heavy financial burden involved. The man pays a substantial bride price in the first place, and upon divorce, the standard contract requires him to meet an even larger separation payment.

Turning to the tribal systems found in Jordan, structurally, the tribe (or at times only its subsections) may be described as a territorial group with pyramidal and segmentary patterns. The significance of the pyramidal pattern is that there is an overall vertical organization of the tribe, not just a series of horizontal units with the same general identity. But the Jordanian tribe is also inherently segmentary: Each segment at each level has a separate identity and a degree of power and authority of its own. Coupling the two concepts, pyramidal and segmentary, indicates that the tribe is organized in an ascending series of segments, each a political and social group at some time and in some events. Thus, each unit at a certain structural level automatically contains all those groups below it. There is no real leadership hierarchy connecting the groups; instead, for example, the shaykh of one of the subsections is in turn the shaykh of the section of which it is a part; similarly, the shaykh of one of the sections is shaykh of the tribe.

As a consequence of internecine fights among tribal sections, tribes, and tribal confederations and of natural demography, the structure is not always so clear-cut and discrete. Over the generations, tribes or tribal sections segment. Thus, at times, a new section forms and splits off from an old section but remains under the umbrella of the larger tribe. Equally, a tribe may split into two parts, sometimes remaining as two sections with the same tribal name and at other times forming totally different tribes. The opposite phenomenon—fusion—also takes place. Two tribes may unite to make one tribe or two sections of separate tribes may split off and then unite to form a separate section of a third tribe or a new tribe of their own.

The highest structural groups in some Jordanian regions are the tribal confederations, which are associations of tribes formed over the centuries. Most tribal political competition is currently at a level lower than the confederations, and they thus have little political or social coherence. But when political activity does rise to this level, in elections, for example, it is evident that they do play a role in the tribal member's loyalty.

Residental Patterns

The Jordanians both historically and currently can be classified as nomadic, seminomadic, semisedentary, and sedentary. These classifications may be considered as four segments of a continuum. The nomads are the "true" bedouin who depend mostly upon camels rather than sheep and goats for their livelihood, live in black (goat hair) tents, and do not settle in permanent houses. The Arab bedouin do not, however, fit the dictionary definition of a nomad. They do not lack a fixed location and just wander from place to place. Rather, a tribe or tribal section has fixed winter and summer camping grounds or areas. At set times of the year, the tribal group will pack up its living quarters and move to its traditional area for the relevant season. The seminomadic people may or may not own camels, but they raise sheep and goats. They tend to live in one area and, unlike the nomads, move only short distances. Both groups rely to a small extent on planting grains. The semi-sedentary tribes cultivate more crops than do the nomads and the seminomads, although they also practice animal husbandry. As a rule, however, only part of a residential group moves with the sheep and goats to new pastures, the remainder staying with the crops. They may or may not live in permanent houses. Finally, the sedentary people live in mud or stone houses and depend on crops for most of their income; what animals they raise are usually under the care of lone herders. Others live in the cities and towns and practice those occupations associated with urban life.

The socioeconomic differentiations cited above reflect the traditional pattern. As is described in the subsections below, these differences have blurred as the country has modernized. The bedouin are now largely settled and resemble the sedentary villagers, albeit with a legacy of bedouin customs and practices. The villager's reliance on agriculture has lessened, while he increasingly enters the labor market, which causes the village population to resemble, to a significant degree, the socioeconomic pattern of urban areas.

Bedouin. Jordan is often described as a bedouin country or, at least, originally a bedouin country. Neither description is accurate, but the bedouin have enjoyed a strong political and cultural role. In the early days of the amirate, the bedouin population was estimated at no more than 40 percent of the total; it was probably less. In 1980, the figure stood at around 5 to 7 percent. Despite the small number, however, the bedouin play a central role in the country, perhaps explaining the misnomer cited above. Politically, the Hashemite regime, once it gained control over the bedouin, relied on their loyalty for crucial support. The army has a significant contingent of bedouin manpower, especially in the more sensitive units and officer ranks. And socioculturally, the East Jordanians often idealize many aspects of bedouin life, saying that the bedouin are the model from which other Jordanian patterns are derived. (Many Palestinians have similar traditions, but direct their comparison to Palestinian bedouin.)

Those who maintain the bedouin life-style largely live in the eastern two-thirds of East Jordan, a desert region of low rainfall that is called the Badia (a word derived from the Arabic word for bedouin, *badu*). At certain times of the year, their encampments are found in the western third of the country, including undeveloped sections of the city of Amman. The bedouin population, as is to be expected, is difficult to estimate. A 1922 estimate put tribal population at 102,950 of a total 225,000.[11] This figure, though, would include people who, although tribal, did not define themselves as bedouin. The correct figure thus was probably in the sixty to seventy-five thousand range. A 1946 estimate indicated normal growth: 99,260 bedouin of a total 433,660 East Jordanians.[12] By the mid-1970s, the Badia population, mostly bedouin (settled or not), was one hundred forty to one hundred fifty thousand out of a population of more than two million.[13] Of this group, it is estimated that far less than fifty thousand are still nomadic, about fifty thousand are at various stages of seminomadism and semisedentarism, and the balance are wholly settled in mud or stone houses.

The tribal pattern described in the previous section holds true for all the bedouin, but the degree of looseness in the structure would strongly correlate to the degree of nomadism of the particular tribe or tribal section. This is because living in nonmobile housing tends to promote a more rigid social structure and vice versa. Additionally, as the bedouin increasingly join the cash economy (significantly through enlistment in the army and settlement for tilled agriculture), socioeconomic dependency, and thus authority patterns, have altered. The primary effect has been to undermine traditional leaders in favor of those based on the new economic patterns.

The most important bedouin tribes are the Huwaytat and the Bani Sukhur. The former was central to the Hashemite-led Arab revolt against the Ottomans during World War I. Other large bedouin tribes are the Bani Atiya, Sirhan, Bani Khalid, and Rwala. The latter is quite a large tribe, but it basically only passes through Jordan on its trek from winter to summer camping grounds. Parts of two Palestinian tribes, Azazma and Jaraba, came over to Jordan during and after 1948.

Certain social patterns are more emphasized among the bedouin, idealized among the settled people, and often claimed as the origin, or pure form, of what is practiced among the settled people. And it is this phenomenon as much as any other that denotes the bedouin contribution to Jordanian culture. It is asserted that bedouin society is strongly characterized by equality. Leaders are recognized but are not given strong authority based on other assets, such as economic power. An example often cited to underline this equality syndrome is that King Hussein is addressed simply by his first name when he visits bedouin encampments; he is treated as the first among equals rather than as royalty. The bedouin also, it is said, take the concept of individual, family, and tribal honor and the defense of this honor to greater lengths than do settled people. The commonly held truth—or myth—is that the bedouin behave as people should, while others' behavior is a pale copy of their practice. In like manner, villagers often state that village tribal structure is just a secondary derivation of the bedouin tribe, and many villagers claim roots in a half-forgotten bedouin past. It is quite often argued that the Arabic language as spoken by the bedouin is the purest and that their poetry is of the highest quality. One finds among all Jordanians both a bedouin dish called *mansif* (lamb cooked in reconstituted dried yogurt) and the bedouin-style coffee. Finally, when a villager or a townsman speaks of the bedouin, he may use the term *badu* or simply say *al-arab*, implying that the bedouin are the true Arabs, from whom all Arab qualities are derived.

The bedouin relationship to central Jordanian authority has altered considerably since the founding of the state. In the initial years of the amirate, the bedouin attempted to carry on as before, maintaining as much independence as possible from central authority. Their economy retained its base in animal husbandry and camel transport, and they tried to continue collecting protection money from neighbors and travelers. One of their most disruptive traditional practices, though, soon caused the state to pay direct attention to them. This practice was the raid, whereby one bedouin tribe would raid another or semisettled villagers-tribesmen in order to take physical possessions. At times raids would escalate to various levels of fighting and even death, causing turmoil in the desert and the countryside. The mid-1920s saw considerable violence but also government pressure for tribes to sign peace treaties among themselves. In 1930, Major John Bagot Glubb (later to become General Sir John Bagot Glubb, or more familiarly, Glubb Pasha) was stationed in Jordan by the British mandatory power, where he quickly established the very effective bedouin desert patrol, a highly mobile force that, along with the presence of the British Royal Air Force, is credited with stopping the raiding practices. Through such activity, the authority of Amir Abdullah's state was projected into the desert. More peaceful traditional practices such as the use of bedouin customary law were not directly challenged but just eroded as modernity encroached on the area.

The recruitment of the bedouin into the armed forces, known as the Arab Legion, was also crucial both for the state and for the bedouin. On the one hand, the ruling Hashemites have come to rely very heavily on the army, which is purposely staffed disproportionately with bedouin recruits. Particularly, one finds bedouin in the strike units, such as artillery and mobile infantry, as well as in the upper levels of the officer ranks. (Men from nonbedouin tribes, especially from the southern half of Jordan, are also generally known for their loyalty and are well

A member of the bedouin-manned desert patrol.

represented in these same sensitive units.) These loyal bedouin elements proved very effective in actively defending the throne in the tumultuous 1950s and during the heavy fighting of September 1970 and its continuation into 1971. On the other hand, the army has changed and continues to change the bedouin. Its broad impact may be noted by the observation that in one major survey, more than one-third of the responding heads of bedouin households were in the military.[14] Thus the military has extensively exposed the bedouin to modernity at various levels of intensity – literacy, health clinics, nutritional practices, new or recent technologies, and the like. Such exposure has, in turn, contributed significantly to bedouin settlement and the decline of nomadic practices.

In the 1970s, the government started paying more direct attention to the welfare of the bedouin as a whole, not just to those in the army. This new activity resulted from the realization that this especially loyal segment of the Jordanian population was not being served as well as the rest of the population. This dearth of attention, which was translated into a lack of clean water and health and other social services, resulted in a lower standard of living than that of the rest of the population. A commonly used gross statistic that demonstrated this disparity is that the estimated life expectancy for the people of the Badia is about fifty years, while the average Jordanian has a life expectancy of sixty years.[15]

In response to this condition, the government invested disproportionately greater resources in the bedouin region. Clinics and schools were built or expanded in a number of areas, and certain feeding programs through international voluntary agencies were commenced. Perhaps more important, the government embarked on a number of measures to improve the environment in which the bedouin live. Very salient in this effort is the provision of water resources through such projects as renovation of the old Roman water cisterns, improvement of springs and drilling of deep wells, and construction of small dams to collect water runoff from mountains and water conveyors to move water to where it can be used. In addition to these activities, the government undertook a series of resettlement schemes – about fourteen by 1980 – whereby families are encouraged to settle on land given or sold to them. In these schemes, considerable farming advice and free or concessional inputs were provided.[16] By means of these comprehensive projects, the central government has succeeded in settling or contributing to the settling of thousands of heretofore nomadic families.

This reorientation of bedouin economics and the basis of their livelihoods has become all the more necessary as the truck displaces their camel transportation income and the central authority's law and order displaces their raiding and protectionism role. In sum, the unique bedouin way of life is being heavily undermined by the changes introduced in the twentieth century.

30

Villagers. Villagers of Jordan today largely call themselves *fellahs* (tillers of the soil, peasants), which reflects the historical difference between their life-styles and those of the bedouin and the urban dwellers. The key distinction is not that they live in villages, but that their primary economic activity is farming the land, and if they practice animal husbandry, in contrast to the bedouin, they do so in a more sedentary manner. Also unlike the bedouin, the *fellahs* did not and do not own camels, but they were and are proud horsemen. The construction of fixed houses rather than tents came about largely when civil order was established in the countryside. Thus, in the mid-nineteenth century, when the Ottomans exercised virtually no control in southern Jordan, in Karak district, for example, only four sites with permanent houses could be found. By the mid-1920s, after more than thirty years of central government presence, thirty-five villages had been built; today there are around eighty. The lack of villages during this earlier period did not mean lack of population. Rather the people lived in tents, being quite prepared to decamp and seek security if a threat appeared. This was the pattern in southern Jordan. In the more northern region around Irbid, the Ottomans had a greater degree of control, and consequently regular villages were more dense.

The tribal and family structure holds for the villagers. Significant variations, however, may be found. In the northern section, the tribe is much smaller and as such is often termed the clan. It generally ranges in size from three hundred to a thousand individuals. In the southern part of the country, although small tribes exist, it is not uncommon to find tribes of up to three to four thousand members. If a tribe were to grow larger than that, the centrifugal forces inherent within it would cause it to break into separate tribes. In earlier days, the tribe was central to protection and economic welfare, and leadership was strongly based on its structure. During the contemporary period, competing systems have arisen, e.g., government, army, and business, and they are often central to economic questions. Consequently, leadership may be based on one of the newer structures, on the tribe, or on both. As a result, the importance of the tribe has lessened.

Formerly the *fellahs'* economy was definitely land-based—cultivating grains and husbanding animals along with trade of these products with neighbors. Today the picture is quite different. In one recent village study, the occupational breakdown was as follows: 39 percent farmers, 28 percent military, 30 percent other nonagriculture (e.g., laborers, masons, and civil servants), and 2 percent retired.[17] Phenomenally, close to half the labor force worked outside the village, namely all those in the military and most of those in the other nonagricultural categories. This pattern, although not exact, is typical of most villages in

Table 3.1: Rural Facilities and Services in Jordan

Facility/Service	1974-75	1980-81	Change	% of Change
Boys Secondary Schools	40	101	+ 61	+153
Girls Secondary Schools	24	46	+ 22	+ 92
Boys Preparatory Schools	347	420	+ 73	+ 21
Girls Preparatory Schools	283	382	+ 99	+ 35
Boys Elementary Schools	650	723	+ 73	+ 11
Girls Elementary Schools	637	704	+ 67	+ 11
Health Clinics	241	314	+ 73	+ 30
MCH (Mother Child Health Clinics)	20	41	+ 21	+105
Improved Water Supply	328	542	+214	+ 65
Agricultural Guide Centers	34	60	+ 26	+ 76
Veterinary Services	8	9	+ 1	+ 13
Cooperatives	63	192	+129	+205
Post Offices or Branches	480	527	+ 47	+ 10
Electrification*	49	329	+280	+571
Community Center Buildings	43	94	+ 51	+119
Social Service Programs				
Child Feeding (Pre-School)	75	98	+ 23	+ 31
Kindergarten	29	75	+ 46	+159
Sewing/Knitting	39	64	+ 25	+ 64
Village Councils**	196	222	+ 26	+ 13
Municipal Councils**	57	76	+ 19	+ 33

Source: "CARE Rural Community Survey Data" - a joint project of CARE, Jordan, the Ministry of Municipal, Rural, Environmental Affairs, Government of Jordan, and USAID/Jordan, kindly provided to the author by CARE Country Director (Jordan) Ralph B. Montee in private correspondence, February 16, 1981

* Rural electrification data include facilities started but not yet completed.

** The actual number for 1980-1981 is greater.

East Jordan. This altered economic structure directly affects the contemporary socioeconomic pattern, with its attendant erosion of traditional leadership and formation of new leadership based on modern skills, ability to relate to the government, and relationship to the nontraditional private sector. Some villages have entirely changed their economic base; they now focus their economic systems on newly developed or developing industries, such as phosphate and potash extraction, cement plants, and light manufacturing and construction.

The provision of services in the villages has increased significantly since the 1960s, often with the direct participation and/or initiative of the villages. Table 3.1 presents a relatively comprehensive picture of what was extant in 1980–1981 and the extent of growth in the previous five to six years. As is evident from the data, conditions in the rural areas have improved considerably if not dramatically in even this short period.

More than 70 percent of the villages now have schools, and most of the rest are acceptably close to villages with schools; almost all villages have clinics or are near villages that do; although only 10 percent of the villages are now electrified, a major development project is scheduled to be completed by 1990 that will provide power to most villages.[18] The greatest problem is the availability of an uncontaminated supply of potable water, which only 60 percent of the villages enjoy. (Water, as noted previously, is an especially serious problem for Jordan.) Although these data are relatively positive as compared to those for many developing countries, it should be pointed out that clinics are not always adequately staffed and education is not always appropriate for the students' future lives, again not an uncommon problem in the developing world.

This general improvement in the rural areas is due to a series of factors. Most salient, perhaps, is the general upward movement of the economy, especially since the mid-1970s, and the remittances from Jordanians abroad, which partially flow to the villages. Second, villagers have become increasingly aware of potential projects that may provide needed services that they may obtain if they petition the government. Notably, if a village organizes and builds a school or clinic, by law the government is required to provide a teacher or medicines and at least visiting medical personnel. Not surprisingly, politics becomes involved; the tribes or families with the strongest connections in Amman often acquire government-provided services for their villages sooner than less well-connected villages. Third, the government under its multiyear plans undertakes to spread these services among the villages. They were included in the five-year plan ending in 1980 but significantly increased in in quantity and quality in the five-year plan starting in 1981.

Fourth, an important contribution to this rural development has been the participation of foreign voluntary organizations in cooperation with the Jordanian Ministry of Municipal, Rural, and Environmental Affairs (MIMREA). The most notable of all these efforts is the U.S. organization CARE's joint program with MIMREA, which has "carried out projects in 40% of the 900 plus rural communities and small towns on the East Bank over the past ten years." And, most laudably, community participation in the projects is quite high: "Local government and communities [contributions] now average 50% to 60% of the total project value." CARE also works "with the Ministry of Social Development to expand social programs in the rural areas through community centers run by local charitable or social societies which provide kindergarten and day care, pre-school child nutrition, sewing and knitting, adult education, etc."[19] Thus, as a consequence of these combined efforts, starting with the communities themselves, but also including the government and foreign organizations, the quality of rural life has been enhanced and the radical shift to the urban areas has definitely been slowed.

Village organization varies considerably. As has been noted, leadership based on tribe and family exists, and the attributes of such leaders are altering due to economic changes and the increasing importance of access to government. A more formal leader, the *mukhtar*, has considerable importance, especially in villages without village or municipal councils. The *mukhtar*, of whom there are two or three per village, is elected by the village families and confirmed by the central government. He is in an ambiguous position, for he is at the service of his tribe or extended families and of the central government, and his obligations may conflict. When selecting the *mukhtar*, the family heads look for an honest man who is respected who has time to devote to the job. If a local tribal leader wants the office, he may have it, but often he does not want it because of the time constraints and conflicts inherent in the position. Although the *mukhtars* do not replace the other leaders, they are pivotal because their office includes authenticating numerous official papers on behalf of the people, recording births and deaths and where people live, accompanying the police on any official business, and being a key person with respect to government programs in the village.

If a village or municipal council exists in a village, however, the role of the *mukhtar* is diminished because the council and its head replace the *mukhtar* in many of the village's dealings with government programs. Villages with a population of more than three thousand may have a municipal rather than a village council. The advantage is that a municipality has more authority in taxation and spending than does a village council. Municipal and village councils have enjoyed only mixed success in Jordan. Essentially they are alien institutions introduced into a traditional setting. The allocation of authority and resources through this structure has often conflicted with local sociopolitical norms, paralyzing the municipalities until the central government intervened. This mixed, somewhat negative pattern was broken with the municipal elections of 1976, when a majority of men who were more educated (often technically) and less traditionally oriented was elected to the municipal councils. This change was a result of the broad educational progress and general efforts at development in the country and the effects of these trends on the desires, perceptions, and outlook of the people. Although problems still exist, it is generally reported that the municipal council and village council systems were working relatively smoothly, albeit not without normal problems, in the latter half of the 1970s.

A certain tension exists with respect to decision making on local development issues. On the one hand, the central government and its personnel are quite development-oriented, make decisions based on development criteria, and control the requisite resources for development. Although they wish to promote local initiative and participation, often their development goals take precedence, and they appear to con-

Palestinian refugee children overlooking a refugee camp in the West Bank.

trol significant aspects of local decision making at the village level, but especially at the regional level. On the other hand, the village people wish to have greater influence and authority concerning decisions affecting their villages. The central government is well aware of this problem and is trying to alleviate it (see Chapters 4 and 6).

Palestinian Camps. A little more than 10 percent of Jordan's population lives in the UNRWA-managed camps, a human settlement pattern that came into being in Jordan in the post-1948 period and was reinforced in the post-1967 period. As mentioned previously, the Palestinian camp population is perhaps the most disgruntled segment of the Jordanian population. The very fact of living in a camp creates a separate psychology and a concentration of despair and/or anger. Contributing to this separate status is the camp population's anomalous position in Jordan. On the one hand, the camp residents live in UNRWA-provided housing, at one time largely tents, but now mostly two-room fixed shelters, and are provided essential services by the UNRWA, namely health care, rations, sanitation, social welfare, and education. (Some of these UNRWA services are provided to Palestinian refugees who do not live in the camps as well.) On the other hand, they are Jordanian citizens, with the rights, privileges, and obligations of citizenship. Thus, while receiving UNRWA government-style services, they must also relate to the Jordanian authorities through the *mukhtar* system, similar to that of the villages, and they see Jordanian authority visibly in the camp in the form of police posts and security operations.

A factor that helps to alleviate the potential anomie of camp residents, but also reinforces their ties to their lost villages or town quarters and thus to Palestine, is that individual camps tend to be made up of families from certain towns, villages, or neighboring villages of pre-1948 Palestine. In this manner, a certain continuity was retained in the refugees' social relationships, and the potential for the growth of solidarity exists. Still another important factor affecting the outlook of the camp resident is the physical location of the refugee camp. Some are just sections of major cities or towns such as Amman, Zarqa, and Irbid. These camps blend into the urban areas and are often indistinguishable from similar poor sections of town. Numerous other camps are in rural areas, creating a certain isolation for their inhabitants, especially as they do not own the surrounding land. Compared to the landless rural-based refugees, the urban camp residents obviously have distinctly enhanced opportunities for employment close to their homes.

Urban Areas. The line distinguishing urban settlement patterns from rural ones is utlimately arbitrary. From a definitional standpoint, the distinction is usually made on the basis of multiplicity of functions and size. In this short work, for convenience, we shall use size as the sole criterion: Settlements of 10,000 inhabitants and above will be defined as urban. On this basis, using the 1979 census, 1,349,034 of the country's 2,152,273 people, or 63 percent, are urban, an extremely high proportion in a developing country. This number is found in nineteen urban localities; the two largest – and neighboring – localities alone claim more than 863,000 people.

The towns are the center of economic activity such as commerce and trade as well as light manufacturing and processing, usually food processing. Also typically, the town is the center for government, where the governor or his lieutenant resides, where branches of the central government's departments are found, where certain decisions affecting the surrounding villages are made. The urban areas are central to the introduction of modernity, being the first places to have schools, health facilities, access to various communication forms and higher technologies; people who have mastered the attendant skills tend to live in these areas. Within this context, the larger towns such as Irbid and Zarqa have developed considerable diversity and a certain sophistication. Unlike their smaller sister towns, they have an industrial base as well as postsecondary educational facilities, most notably a university near Irbid.

An Amman vista.

The greater Amman urban area deserves special mention because of its size, uniqueness to Jordan, and importance as the capital and center of commerce, industry, and cultural life. Unlike the ancient capitals of other Arab countries, Amman is a new town. Before 1875, what is now Amman consisted solely of the ruins of the once prosperous Roman city of Philadelphia. Popular lore has it that Circassians settled the area in 1871; certainly they had built a village there by the 1880s. Over the years, it developed a minor reputation as a commercial center that was much enhanced by the completion of the northern section of the Hijaz railroad, which passed only 3 miles (5 kilometers) east of the village in 1905. The status of Amman was truly settled in 1921 when Amir Abdullah, after trekking around his new amirate, established himself in Amman and made it his capital. Population growth, however, was slow; the population reached only about twenty thousand in the early 1940s.[20] Subsequent to 1948 and the influx of Palestinians, however, growth was extremely rapid: 108,000 in 1952, 648,587 in 1979, with the total urban area, including Zarqa, approaching a million. Although rural-to-urban migration has certainly contributed to population growth, the great influxes of Palestinian refugees accounted for the greatest growth and caused the city to become largely Palestinian.

Most of Amman is located on a series of rather steep hills, locally called *jabals*. Houses and small apartment buildings seem to be clinging to the sides of these *jabals*. Only in the new sections of the city, now stretching far from the center, are found flat areas or gentle slopes covered with various forms of residential structures.

Due to the boom conditions often afflicting Amman and the seemingly endless influx of people, capped most recently by the temporary arrival of twenty to thirty thousand Lebanese at the height of the Lebanese civil war, pressure on housing and basic infrastructure has been continually severe. One aspect of this boom has, ironically, benefited the bedouin, because they owned much of the land on which Amman is now built and have sold it at very high prices. And prices or rents for houses and apartments have consistently stayed high, especially as Jordanian law requires rents to remain constant as long as a renter occupies his apartment. The extraordinary housing prices have forced some groups to seek more economical alternatives. A popular one is for groups of professionals, army officers, municipal workers, civil servants, and the like to form cooperatives and jointly purchase land (often in somewhat remote areas away from services) and build relatively standard tract houses. Another housing phenomenon is that often various units of extended families tend to live together despite uneven incomes, causing a definite mixture of classes in various quarters. That is not to say that some quarters or *jabals* are not characterized by either poverty or riches—very definitely some are.

Water and sewage services are not consistently provided. Only one-quarter of the houses are attached to the sewer system, the balance using cesspools that must be periodically pumped dry or flow into the streets. Also, only three-quarters of the houses have running water, which, because it is usually supplied only once a week or less (residents ordinarily store water in tanks on their roofs), is at times inadequate. The quarter of the population without piped water and those with inadequate supplies purchase water from the city via tank truck or from commercial suppliers at much higher rates.[21]

Due to its newness, Amman does not have the rich traditions of classical Arab capital cities such as Damascus, Baghdad, Cairo, or Rabat. It has no *suq* (traditional market) to rival the markets of these cities nor the artisans and their traditions to go along with them. Rather the city exudes newness, with shining off-white buildings dotting the landscape. It lacks local roots; Palestinians, refugees and nonrefugees alike, are the majority, and because of their recent arrival, most keep their earlier identities, culture, and values. Thus, very few people living in Amman will say they are from Amman. Recently, especially with many Jordanians leaving for the oil-rich countries and creating a void in the labor market, the influx of villagers, with their rural values, has increased.

On the positive side, most people in Amman have easy access to schools and health services as well as news media. Television is relatively new; radio and newspapers have been in existence longer. Other forms of communication, such as buses, taxis, and airplanes, are readily available. The telex and telephone systems have been overly taxed in the recent city expansion, but were significantly expanded in 1980–1981.

A final note should be made about the urban bias of services and resources, a problem that has recently become a serious concern of the government. The government is of course centered in Amman, the capital, and the larger towns have branches of the government departments. But the advantages of urban areas do not stop there. The urban literacy rate is 74 percent, versus 55 percent in the rural areas. The Amman governorate, which claims the two largest cities of Amman and Zarqa, has 56 percent of the population but 85 percent and 71 percent of the large and small industries respectively. The governorates of Amman and Balqa, with only 63 percent of the population, consume 85 percent of Jordan's electricity. Urban incomes also greatly surpass those of rural areas. In the Amman governorate, the 1973 averages were 603 Jordanian dinars (JD) and 381 JD respectively, and in the country as a whole, the comparison was 572 JD versus 361 JD (1 JD = $3.35). In both cases, rural income was just 63 percent of urban income. With this disparity, and the perception that jobs are to be found in urban areas, it is not surprising that in the 1961–1979 period, the annual population growth rate of urban areas (5.37 percent) exceeded that of rural areas (4.85 percent).[22] Recognizing that the urban and Amman bias is a problem, the government now provides tax incentives for the establishment of industry outside Amman and is setting up the previously noted regional councils, made up of local leaders, which will take on certain planning functions and provide a means for sharing some aspects of decision making with people outside Amman.

Socioeconomic Stratification

Hard data on Jordanian socioeconomic strata do not exist, but one may describe them in the following general terms. In the rural areas, although strata based on such differentials as income, education, job, and status definitely exist, these differences are mitigated by the cross-strata ties of the tribe and extended family as well as by the ideology (not always realized) of equality among the bedouin and to a lesser degree among villagers. Although certain exceptions stand out, as a rule the more wealthy in the rural areas do not ostentatiously exhibit their wealth. In urban areas, especially Amman and Zarqa, contrasts among the strata are more glaring. They are easily seen in housing: Sections of Amman are filled with fine, large houses and fancy cars in a display of conspicuous consumption. Similarly, the slightly lower, but still well-to-do, strata enjoy the luxury of fine apartments and other signs of wealth.

At the other extreme, many people are found occupying one- or two-room houses, usually without sewer connections and cars, often without water. These are the refugee poor or the rural families flocking into Amman in pursuit of jobs. Such rooms are occasionally occupied by a group of laborers from a village, hoping to return with enough funds to reestablish themselves in their village. Above them are the more skilled laborers and the small shopowners, some of whom may have called Amman home for at least ten or twenty years. At the next level are white-collar workers, either in the government or the growing private sector, who proudly distinguish themselves from the lower group. At the top are the groups described above: higher-level people in government and the private sector, professionals, industrialists, and large land-owners. And many are bringing their wealth back from the oil-rich countries, establishing themselves in the upper strata of Amman.

RELIGION

Jordan is overwhelmingly a Muslim nation. More than 90 percent of the population adhere to that faith, and virtually all follow the Sunni (as opposed to the Shiʿa) school of Islam. Islam is recognized as the official religion of the country, and the state provides or regulates the means through which the Muslim religious structure reaches the people. Thus, the government Ministry of Awqaf, Islamic Affairs and Holy Places pays the salaries of religious personnel and most religiously learned men (ulama), maintains the mosques, and supports Islamic religious schools. The ministry also administers the sharia (or Muslim religious law) courts that, like their Christian counterparts, adjudicate personal-status cases as well as legal matters having to do with the awqaf (religious endowments).

The Hashemite regime claims direct descendancy from the Prophet Muhammad. This special relationship to the revealer of Islam[23] lends political legitimacy to the Hashemite family and King Hussein, especially among the bedouin and, to a lesser degree, among the fellahs of the villages. Additionally, King Hussein and his grandfather Amir (later King) Abdullah were careful to maintain close relations with the ulama, attempting to co-opt rather than alienate them as was the practice in some neighboring Middle Eastern states. In a like manner, the government actively encourages the building of mosques, especially after considerable funding for this purpose became available from Saudi Arabia in the post-1973 oil boom period. And the government has for some time made its communication services, notably radio and television and some journals, available for Muslim sermons, teaching, and reading of the Muslim holy book, the Quran. On a more political level, well preceding the period of broadly increased Islamic fervor in the Middle East, King

40

PEOPLE

Table 3.2:   Jordanian Literacy by Selected Age Group and Sex

in 1974

Percent Literate			Age Group
Male	Female	Total	
86	80	83	12 - 14
74	30	50	35 - 39
28	5	18	65 & older
78	52	65	12 & older

Source: Adapted from the Jordan Statistical Bureau,
Multi-Purpose Household Survey, 1974.

Hussein found a modus vivendi with the Muslim Brotherhood, a strong fundamentalist and orthodox Muslim party that exists throughout the Arab Middle East, to the extent that it did not oppose him in the turbulent 1950s and supported him during the bleak 1970-1971 period. Consequently, as Islamic fervor gained strength in the Middle East in the late 1970s, early 1980s, and presumably beyond, King Hussein's regime has not felt the pressures or threats to its existence from that source as have neighboring countries.

Nevertheless, there have been notable manifestations of this Islamic fervor since the late 1970s, albeit more of an increase in certain practices rather than new practices. For example, one observes more women dressing in a conspicuously conservative manner. Thus, not the black robe and veil of yesteryear, but long coat and head scarf in a muted color are a common sight. Radio and television are giving more air time than previously to religiously oriented programs. During Ramadan, the holy month for Muslims, the required fasting during daylight hours is more strictly observed. Most restaurants are closed and one rarely observes people smoking in public. This description of a variation on an old pattern should not be taken to mean that Jordanians have forsaken some of the practices adopted from the West; rather they are blended in a slightly new way into the overall culture.

EDUCATION

The best way to examine education in Jordan is to describe the phenomenal growth of this sector and the greatly increased ability of the country to provide educational opportunities for its population. Table 3.2 shows the rapid increase in literacy by age group. Thus, of those over

Table 3.3:   Pupils Enrolled in Schools

by Percent of Selected Age Groups in 1974

Males	Females	Total	Age Groups
98	93	96	10 year olds
60	71	66	16 year olds
24	15	19	20 year olds

Source: Adapted from Jordan Statistical Bureau, Multi-Purpose Household Survey, 1974.

sixty-five, only 18 percent were literate in 1974, while the young teenagers enjoyed 83 percent literacy. Importantly, women are rapidly catching up with men. Of the sixty-five plus group, men were five times more literate than women, but their advantage drops to a mere 6 percent for the early teenage group.

The first twelve years of schooling are relatively standard. The primary cycle (the first six years) and the preparatory cycle (the next three years) are compulsory and include the typical array of courses in reading, writing, arithmetic, history, geography, science, and religion (not required of non-Muslims). The secondary cycle leads to the *tawjihi* certificate (high school diploma); it has two major streams—humanities and sciences. The next phase of the regular system is the universities, of which there are now two, the University of Jordan, near Amman, and Yarmouk University, near Irbid. In addition to this regular cycle, technical schools are now being developed and attract thousands of students. Enrollment rates for 1974 at selected age levels are indicated in Table 3.3. The figures in this table indicate that more than 95 percent of the school-age population is benefiting from the basic compulsory cycle, but the proportion drops to two-thirds at the secondary cycle and one-fifth at the postsecondary cycle (university students and some technical institute students).

Each of these levels also has its own peculiar characteristics. As with all of Jordan, the educational system is not uniform. Only 70 percent of the pupils attend government schools, with 22 percent in UNRWA schools and 8 percent in private ones. From the early 1950s, as is obvious from the literacy figures, the government (and the UNRWA) promoted the rapid growth of schools—and this policy succeeded to the extent that by the 1960s the demand for teachers far exceeded the supply. To fill this crucial gap, the government rapidly expanded the teacher training colleges, increasing the output from 350 graduates in the late 1960s to 2,900 in 1977. In addition, the UNRWA developed an innova-

King Hussein presenting diplomas at the University of Jordan.

tive in-service teacher training program to upgrade the teachers hired during rapid expansion of its school system in the 1950s. This successful program was copied by Jordan – and by numerous other Arab countries in subsequent years.

Another major problem has been the emphasis on the humanities. Only recently have students started studying science in larger numbers and, as is noted below, in the 1970s technical education, a much needed skill in Jordan and the Middle East, acquired considerable popularity.

With respect to university education, in the 1981–1982 academic year twelve thousand students were enrolled at the University of Jordan, and at the new Yarmouk University there were five thousand students. Enrollment for the latter was projected to reach twenty thousand by 1990. In addition, in 1979–1980 about forty-five thousand students were studying outside Jordan, mostly in the Arab world but a few thousand each in Western and Eastern countries. Both Jordanian universities are relatively young; the University of Jordan was founded in the 1960s and Yarmouk University in the 1970s. Notably, both, unlike most Arab Middle Eastern universities, have adopted and adapted the U.S., rather than the European, university structure – course credits, lectures, seminars, research papers, frequent exams, and the like. And both offer the normal range of degrees in arts and sciences, education, business, medicine,

Students at a technical institute.

agriculture, and engineering. Most observers consider these two institutions to be the best state-supported universities in the Arab Middle East.
Recently, however, considerable societal and governmental pressure has
come to bear on the universities to increase rapidly their enrollments,
and this aim is being partially realized. Some feel that this action has
seriously undermined the quality of education. Interestingly, when the
government decided to build the universities, it sited them a few miles
from the cities, not only so that they would have sufficient land, but also
presumably so that the students would be somewhat isolated and unable
to cause riotous disruptions in heavily populated areas. A new university
is slated for Mu'ta, near the provincial town of Karak, which will be
specially designed to educate personnel for government and military service.

Traditionally, technical education has been shunned in the Middle
East, and Jordan is no exception. Socially, working with one's hands was
frowned upon, white-collar jobs being greatly preferred. Attitudes are
now changing, and young men and women are increasingly demanding
such education and are now finding places in the various institutions.
The greatest incentive for this change is most probably that technically
trained people can easily find employment at decent wages. The following data indicate the extent of the growth in this form of education: (1)

Prior to 1970, there were only two technical trade schools (one run by the UNRWA, one by a foreign charity); by 1978, there were an additional eighteen government-run institutes (twelve for boys, six for girls) with an enrollment of 3,660 in two-year courses; (2) in 1970, no adult technical educational classes existed; but by 1976, 2,500 were enrolled in eight- to ten-month courses; and (3) by 1978, 1,000 students were enrolled in six three-year colleges for staff nurses.[24]

Given this rapid expansion, one would think that employment would be a distinct problem. Indeed, up to the early 1970s, this was the case. After the mid-1970s, however, the opposite has become the rule. In many sectors, there are absolute shortages of trained manpower because the oil-rich countries are rapidly siphoning off many skilled people and because of Jordan's own economic boom, which began in the mid-1970s.

A new development in nonformal education was the establishment in the 1970s of the Haya Arts Center. Located in an upper-middle-class section of Amman, it offers facilities for children's arts and a fine library. More important, it has embarked on a program of distributing children's books throughout the countryside. In 1980, it cooperated with eighty libraries run by municipalities and various kinds of community-based societies. In this manner, it is providing an important supplement to the standard formal educational systems.

We should note that education occupies a special place and is given a special emphasis in Jordan. It is often observed that Jordan lacks natural physical resources but has a rich abundance of human resources that, if they are to contribute to growth and development, must benefit broadly from education. In practical terms, this means that families make very considerable sacrifices to educate their children, and from the government standpoint, state resources must be and are heavily invested in this sector. Palestinians value education at yet another level. They say that education is an all-important asset that, once acquired, can never be taken away from an individual—unlike land, houses, and businesses, which they or their fathers and mothers lost in Palestine.

CULTURE

Kamel Abu Jaber's insightful and sensitive *The Jordanians and the People of Jordan* draws the two salient themes in the culture of the country. First,

culturally our people waver between what is and what was. The past, glorious as it was, rightly holds its own attractions, but the present has just as good attractions and the future holds limitless ones. A person's soul is torn between all these possibilities and probabilities. That is why it is not uncommon to find in the same person several cultural personalities. The mood may be oriental, western or somewhere in-between and one is responsive to all these moods; not out of blind or superficial imitation, but because of a genuine appreciation of both the traditional and the new. And it is thus that every Jordanian lives in a variety of worlds; old and new and in-between. The choice and diversity is bewildering and rich. . . . [Second,] Jordan is an extension of the surrounding Arab culture. In a way, it is part and parcel of that culture, and thus difficult to differentiate from it except for the very discriminating and the discerning. Yet in fact local variants do exist.[25]

These variations are contributed by the various minorities. Thus, Assyrians enjoy distinctive food and music of forgotten times; the Circassians have their Fantasia dances and quite different mode of dress; and Christian churches carry on centuries-old chants and rituals. All these minority cultural practices are virtually identical to those of brother minorities in neighboring countries. Many of the traditional crafts are basically imitative of ancient patterns, open to little or no innovation. Thus, wooden utensils, metal (mostly copper and brass) dishes, bowls and pots, and various forms of glass exhibit ageless utilitarian patterns, but because of the use of modern, often imported replacements, few artisans still practice the traditional crafts – and much is imported from Syria. The bedouin and some villagers stand out in this area with their distinctive heavy cloth saddle bags, simple silver-clad knives, and striped wool carpets. Traditional clothing, especially women's dress with its cross-stitch patterns of varying degrees of elaborateness, clearly identifies the individual's village or tribe in East Jordan or Palestine. But more and more often, both men and women are adopting Western-style clothes – more in urban than in rural areas and more among younger than older people.

Under traditional Islam, representational art was forbidden. Thus geometric design, ornamentation, and calligraphy flourished and representational art languished until this century. Today an active school of painting, using oriental and Western motifs, exists; there is even a member of the royal family, Princess Wijdan, who participates.

The past, present, and future of which Abu Jaber spoke are most strongly represented for the visitor by clothing – the visual – and music – the audible. The rich variation of village styles mixed with modern dress has its musical counterpart. During the course of a day one may hear characteristic bedouin songs of the desert and war, perhaps accompanied by stringed *rababas* and drums; modern Arab music and singing of the late Um Kalthum or Sabah, famed throughout the Arab world; men and women singing, clapping and dancing to *debke*, belly dance, or other Arab dance variations; Western popular and classical music in the home; and "disco." As in centuries past, the *muazzin* of the mosque

An Amman street scene.

beautifully sings out the call to prayers, a traditional rendering of the Quran in human voice, five times a day—and the chants of the Christian churches, whether in Greek, Arabic, or Latin, are ageless musical forms commonly found in Jordan.

Less evident to the visitor is the most rigorous of Arab cultural forms, the literature of prose, poetry, and conversation. Arabs generally, and Jordanians are certainly no exception, idealize their language and honor those who can use it well. Some even go so far as to say, somewhat hyperbolically, that language and expression among the Arabs become so important that they are mistaken for action. Abu Jaber wrote that Jordanians (and other Arabs) "feel that if they express how they feel others will understand and injustices will be righted."[27] Arabs generally assert that the Quran is the perfect expression of the Arabic language and the general pattern from which the language is drawn. Certainly this traditional classical linguistic mode of writing is broadly found in literature. Modern classical Arabic is equally found in the newspapers and on the radio and television. From this standard form, one variously hears numerous gradations down to local dialects or accents, the degree of use of the local variation often inversely correlating to the level of an individual's education. Prose appears in all the forms, although purists are highly critical of any writing not in the classical form. Poetry follows more stylized patterns, as poetry often does in the West.

From an organizational standpoint, culture is promoted in two ways. On the private front, quite frequently people join together and form clubs, often termed "Cultural and Sports Club" or the like. Using these as a base, the individuals and groups undertake studies, readings, and the dissemination of cultural forms. On the public front, the government, usually through the Ministry of Information and Culture, sponsors and encourages the arts through subsidies, organization of shows and expositions, and visits by foreign artists and performers.

In sum, Jordanian culture, like that of many developing countries, is an evolving mixture of the old and the new as well as of East and West. The result is a workable whole that gives Jordanians the opportunity to live and express themselves in a variety of modes. This culture is distinctly part of the larger Arab culture, drawing richness from it as well as donating traditional and, increasingly, modern contributions to it.

NOTES

1. There was a housing count in 1952 that, although not a census, certainly added to the reliability of statistical data after that date.

2. Munib al-Mady and Sulayman Musa, *Taʾrikh al-ʾUrdun fi al-Qarn al-ʿIshrin* [History of Jordan in the twentieth century] (Amman?, 1959), pp. 311, 448.

3. Reference here is *only* to Palestinians, refugees or otherwise, who were in the West and East Banks of Jordan. Hundreds of thousands of other Palestinians went to Gaza, Lebanon, and Syria, and still others remain in Israel.

4. Israel, Central Bureau of Statistics, *Statistical Abstract of Israel* (Jerusalem, various years).

5. *Report of the Commissioner-General of the United Nations Relief and Works Agency for Palestine Refugees in the Near East (1 July 1979–30 June 1980)* (New York: United Nations, 1980), Table 4, p. 64.

6. Shaul Mishal, *West Bank/East Bank, the Palestinians in Jordan, 1949–1967* (New Haven, Conn.: Yale University Press, 1978), pp. 2–5; Daniel Lerner, *The Passing of Traditional Society* (New York: Free Press, 1958), pp. 306–310; Naseer H. Aruri, *Jordan: A Study in Political Development (1921–1965)* (The Hague: Martinus Nijhoff 1972), p. 36.

7. Lerner, *Passing of Traditional Society*, p. 306.

8. Raphael Patai, *The Kingdom of Jordan* (Princeton, N.J.: Princeton University Press, 1958), p. 22.

9. R. D. McLaurin (ed.), *The Political Role of Minority Groups in the Middle East* (New York: Praeger Publishers, 1979), p. 274. In addition, twenty thousand Lebanese Christians were temporarily in the country during the Lebanese war.

10. Peter Gubser, *Politics and Change in al-Karak, Jordan* (London: Oxford University Press, 1973), pp. 62–64.

11. al-Mady and Musa, *Ta'rikh al-'Urdun*, p. 311.

12. Ibid., p. 448.

13. Kamel S. Abu Jaber et al., "Socio-Economic Survey of the Badia of Northeast Jordan," unpublished study, Faculty of Economics and Commerce, University of Jordan, June 1976.

14. Ibid., Table 5.

15. Allen Hill, "Population Composition, Mortality and Fertility," in ibid., pp. 10–11.

16. Salah M. Yacoub, "Sedentarization and Settlement of the Nomadic Populations in Selected Countries of the ECWA Region," paper presented at the Ninth World Congress of Sociology, August 1978, pp. 45–56.

17. Richard Antoun, *Low-Key Politics: Local-Level Leadership and Change in the Middle East* (Albany: State University of New York Press, 1979), p. 25.

18. Jarir S. Dajani and Muneera S. Murdock, "Assessing Basic Human Needs in Rural Jordan," mimeographed (Washington, D.C.: United States Agency for International Development, September 1951), passim.

19. "CARE Rural Community Survey Data" (a joint project of CARE, Jordan, the Ministry of Municipal, Rural, Environmental Affairs, Government of Jordan, and USAID/Jordan), kindly provided to the author by CARE Country Director (Jordan) Ralph B. Montee in private correspondence, February 16, 1981.

20. James M. Hacker, *Modern Amman* (Durham: Department of Geography, Durham Colleges, 1960), passim.

21. Jarir S. Dajani, "A Social Soundness Analysis of the Amman Water and Sewerage Systems," mimeographed (Washington, D.C.: United States Agency for International Development, April 1978), passim.

22. Ahmad Malkawi, *Regional Development in Jordan—Some Aspects of the*

Urban Bias (Amman: Royal Scientific Society, 1978), passim. Please note that both growth rates are higher than the natural growth rate due to the large influx of refugees from the West Bank and Gaza Strip in 1967 and a sustained flow in subsequent years.

23. For an excellent short description of Islam, see H.A.R. Gibb, *Muhammadism* (New York: Oxford University Press, 1953).

24. Jordan Ministry of Information, *Training Institutes in Jordan* (Amman, 1978), passim.

25. Kamel Abu Jaber, "The Jordanians and the People of Jordan," unpublished 1980 manuscript (due to be published by the Jordanian Royal Scientific Society), p. 80.

26. Ibid.

4

Economy

Prior to World War I, agriculture was the primary component of the East Bank's economy.[1] Commerce and governmental participation in the economy were minuscule in comparison to that sector, that is until the Hijaz railroad was laid in the area, slightly increasing the importance of commerce. Industry consisted largely of food processing, such as grinding wheat for flour, and cottage handicrafts. During the period between World War I and World War II, there was only slight and gradual economic change. Agriculture retained its paramount position, but the role of government increased with the recruitment of an army and the gradual provision of an infrastructure for health, education, and the like. Industry remained unimportant, as did all but a few nongovernmental services.

The post-1948 period witnessed radical change. With the arrival of the refugees in the East and the occupied (later annexed) West Bank, the economy shifted from one dominated by agriculture to one dominated by services as both the government and the UNRWA sought to meet the needs of the refugees. The central government, officially free of the British mandate, also was attempting to expand its functions and develop the country's infrastructure. The private sector was significantly influenced by the tens of thousands of Palestinians who came to Amman (and to a lesser extent to other areas), bringing with them capital and/or entrepreneurial skills. Not only did these newcomers stimulate the housing sector, but also they applied themselves in the service sector, primarily commerce, causing it to grow rapidly. During the late 1950s and 1960s, another external event added talent to Jordan, albeit at a much slower rate than the refugee flood. This was the Syrian social and economic revolution, which caused two to three hundred thousand people, mostly middle-class, to leave, largely for Lebanon, but also for Jordan. As a result of all these factors, the Jordanian economy experienced a substantial gross national product (GNP) growth rate: 11 percent per year during the 1954–1967 period. It should be remembered that this growth was on a very small initial base, which tends to magnify small absolute increments.

The bleakest period in Jordan's economic history was undoubtedly the years from 1967 through 1973. In 1967, the West Bank was lost, along with its talented people, rich agricultural land, and incomparable tourist attractions – the Christian and Muslim holy sites in and around Jerusalem. In addition, the burden of three hundred thousand more refugees was added to the East Bank. During 1968, 1969, and 1970, Palestinian guerrilla forays against Israel and Israel's military action caused the developing and fruitful agriculture of the Jordan Valley to be curtailed; it almost ceased for a while. The 1970–1971 Jordanian civil war added to Jordan's economic woes, virtually shutting down some economic sectors and causing part of the subsidy awarded to the Jordanian government by oil-producing Arab states in the aftermath of the 1967 Arab-Israeli war to cease. In reaction to the civil war, Syria closed its airspace to Jordan and other Arab countries shunned Jordan. Not until after the 1973 October war and especially the Rabat summit conference of 1974 was Jordan again treated normally from both a political and economic standpoint by the various Arab countries. It is estimated by most economists that Jordan's GNP did not reach its pre-1967 level until 1975–1976, albeit with a different land, resource, and population base.

After the Arab-Israeli October war and the dramatic rise in the price of petroleum, Jordan's economy enjoyed a sustained boom. From 1976 to the time of this writing, gross domestic product (GDP) annual growth in constant prices has been consistently in the 9–12 percent range. This rapid economic growth was a result of several major stimuli. First, despite Jordan's lack of petroleum, its neighbors' seemingly ever-increasing fortunes have rubbed off onto this resource-poor country. As noted earlier, Jordanian citizens are working throughout the oil-producing countries, and the remittances of this group are added to the Jordanian economy. Citizens of these countries, equally, are investing in housing and business in Jordan; they also provide income through tourism. Similarly, on the governmental side, significant monetary transfers have been made by Arab governments to the Jordanian government, both as direct budgetary support and as loans or grants for Jordan's ambitious development program.

Second, what Lebanon lost during its civil war, starting in 1975, Jordan partially gained. Twenty to thirty thousand Lebanese and a few thousand Western residents moved to Jordan in 1975 and 1976 (the majority, but not all, the Lebanese have now left), further stimulating the housing and services boom. In addition, Lebanon ceased to render a number of services it had provided to the oil-producing countries, from banking to commerce to technical services, and no longer served as a summer resort. Some of these activities the Lebanese themselves continued from a Jordanian base, others the Jordanians took over. (Naturally, still others, the majority, shifted to bases in Europe or the petroleum-producing countries.)

Third, the price of phosphate, Jordan's most important export, rose dramatically, and this was followed by a major increase in phosphate production, a project long under way. Fourth, the Jordan Valley returned to agriculture production, which expanded rapidly as the irrigation scheme was repaired and further developed. Fifth, closely related to points three and four, Jordanian development efforts started paying off in a sustained manner. Within these development efforts, it is obvious that one of the major themes has been and is to create an infrastructure so that free enterprise, commerce, and industry can grow. This infrastructure involves not only roads, a port, telephones, and telex and other communications facilities, but also a structure of laws promoting and protecting business and industry as well as the provision of direct investment capital for some of the larger industrial or mining corporations. Although it may not distribute national income equitably, this official policy has certainly stimulated the growth of the private sector.

LABOR FORCE AND GROSS DOMESTIC PRODUCT
BY SECTORS

Labor force statistics for Jordan may be drawn only from the 1961 census and special surveys undertaken in 1974 and 1975, which, unfortunately, are incomplete and partially inaccurate. Fortunately, however, Michael Mazur, in his excellent and analytic *Economic Growth and Development in Jordan*, has provided us with extrapolated data that come as close as possible to accuracy (see Table 4.1). The two sectors that have altered the most are agriculture and services. In the former, we can see the normal decline as agriculture modernizes and people are drawn out of agriculture to urban areas. The growth of services is due largely to the growth of government, primarily the military. Of the labor force of four hundred thirty thousand in Jordan, it is reliably estimated that one hundred thousand are in the army (the size of the army has not been officially revealed), accounting for fully 23 percent of the total. Growth in the number of teachers and other government employees would account for the balance. As compared to other countries, Jordan is low in agricultural labor and high in services. The figure for agriculture is skewed by the presence of a large refugee population as well as by the limited supply of fertile land and water resources; that for services is skewed by the refugee presence and by the overly large military.

Table 4.2 presents a breakdown of the GDP. Overall, it may be noted that GDP has increased between 1973 and 1979 by about 20 percent on an annual basis (in constant prices about 12 percent annually).

Table 4.1: Sectoral Distribution of Development, East
Bank (1961 and 1974-75) and Typical Developing Country

Share in Total Employment (percent)

| | | East Bank | | Typical Developing Country |
		1961	1974-1975	
I.	Primary Production	35	20	50.7
	A. Agriculture	32	18	49.7
	B. Mining	3	2	1.0
II.	Industry	21	18	20.8
	A. Manufacturing	9	8	15.5
	B. Construction	12	10	5.4
III.	Services	45	62	28.5
	A. Transport	4	5	4.1
	B. Trade, Banking, and Insurance	9	9	8.2
	C. Other Services, including the Government and the Army	32	48	16.2
	Total Employment	100	100	100

Source: Michael P. Mazur, Economic Growth and Development in Jordan
          (Boulder, Colorado: Westview Press, 1979), p. 112.

Note: Discrepancies in totals due to rounding.

Per capita income (GDP per capita) in 1979 was 280 JD or $949, a
relatively high figure for a developing country with few resources. From
a sectoral standpoint, growth in mining, manufacturing, and construction is most noteworthy. As with the distribution of labor, GDP is heavily skewed toward the service sector and away from agriculture. Notable
growth in productive aspects of the service sector is evident, namely in
transportation and hotels, both of which are foreign currency earners for
Jordan.

BALANCE OF PAYMENTS

Jordan's balance of trade and its balance of trade and services have
been chronically and radically in deficit, as is demonstrated in Table 4.3.
In 1978, for example, imports of goods were valued at 5.5 times exports
of goods. Considering the trade balance of both goods and services, still
Jordan imported 192,200,000 JD more than it exported. Despite this
severe imbalance in trade of goods and services, two factors strongly

Table 4.2: Gross Domestic Product by Sector

In Millions of JD and % of Year's Total

	1971	%	1973	%	1975	%	1977	%	1979	%
Agriculture	23.9	13.7	17.6	9.2	26.0	9.5	41.7	10.3	48.0	8.0
Industrial	26.0	14.9	24.0	12.6	49.9	18.3	89.1	21.9	118.2	19.6
Manufacturing	(14.1)		(17.2)		(30.5)		(65.1)		(79.6)	
Mining & Quarrying	(2.3)		(4.0)		(16.3)		(19.9)		(30.8)	
Utilities	(2.2)		(2.8)		(3.1)		(4.1)		(7.8)	
Construction	7.4	4.0	15.2	8.0	16.1	5.9	27.0	6.6	43.0	7.1
Services	117.5	67.2	133.7	70.2	180.3	66.2	248.9	61.2	392.8	65.2
Government Services	(43.6)		(46.7)		(65.2)		(84.4)		(112.0)	
Transportation & Communications	(14.6)		(17.9)		(24.9)		(35.9)		(79.0)	
Financial Services	(19.8)		(22.5)		(29.7)		(43.6)		(67.0)	
Commerce, Hotels, & Restaurants	(33.0)		(38.1)		(46.3)		(66.3)		(105.0)	
Other	(6.4)		(8.5)		(14.2)		(18.7)		(29.8)	
Total	174.8		190.5		272.3		406.7		602.0	

Source: Derived from Central Bank of Jordan, Monthly Statistical Bulletin, various years. Percentages are rounded and do not total 100.

Table 4.3: Summary of the Balance of Payments

(In Million JDs)

		1975	1977	1978
A.	Goods, Services, & Transfers	21.5	-2.5	-85.8
	1. Goods & Services (net)	-118.3	-168.3	-192.3
	Trade Balance	-184.1	-270.0	-371.0
	Exports	48.9	68.7	82.1
	Imports	233.0	338.7	453.1
	Services (net)	65.7	202.8	175.7
	Workers Remittances (net)	53.3	139.8	139.4
	Travel, Investment, & Other Services	12.4	63.0	36.3
	2. Transfer Payments	139.8	165.8	106.5
	Private	1.8	-1.1	3.9
	Central Government	138.0	166.9	102.6
	From Arab Governments	105.7	132.3	66.3
	From U.S. Government	22.4	15.6	18.6
	From U.N. Agencies	2.9	17.0	17.8
B.	Capital Account	44.1	50.2	90.9
	Private (net)	6.3	3.8	17.2
	Local Government (net)	0.4	0.0	0.0
	Central Government (net)	37.4	46.4	73.7
C.	Net Errors and Omissions	-18.9	17.0	31.8
D.	Net Total (A, B & C)	46.7	64.7	36.9
E.	Monetary Movements	-46.7	-64.7	-36.9

Source: Central Bank of Jordan, Monthly Statistical Bulletin, various years.

contribute to almost bringing the overall balance of payments out of deficit.[2] First is the growing significance of remittances from Jordanians abroad. These remittances are a new phenomenon, increasing from only 24 million JD in 1974 to 53 million JD in 1975 to 140 million JD in 1978, and it is believed that these are highly understated figures. Second is the transfer payments (see Table 4.4 as well) to the government, a practice that dates back to the mandate period and has continued throughout the period of Jordanian independence. Expectedly, the source of these payments is closely correlated to Jordan's political fortunes as well as the

Table 4.4:   Foreign Receipts of Central Government

(In thousands of JDs)

Source	1975	1977	1979*
Total	116,764	180,713	266,204
1. Budget Support	97,109	122,196	203,234
a. U.S.A.	17,138	14,252	4,545
b. Arab	79,971	107,944	198,689
2. Economic & Technical Assistance	3,500	6	-
3. Development Loans	16,155	58,511	62,970
a) U.K.	1,298	-	7,890
b) West Germany	5,185	11,338	7,474
c) Kuwait	1,079	7,124	6,152
d) I.D.A.	3,765	3,935	6,240
e) U.S.A.I.D.	2,556	13,590	13,046
f) Saudi Arabia**	-	4,000	4,219
g) Qatar	-	-	-
h) Denmark	230	-	-
i) Iran	1,558	3,000	360
j) Republic of China	484	1,200	-
k) Abu-Dhabi	-	2,568	1,000
l) Arab Fund for Economic & Social Development	-	5,896	4,059
m) Iraq	-	3,500	3,100
n) Japan	-	1,500	945
o) Other	-	860	8,475

Source: Central Bank of Jordan,   Monthly Statistical Bulletin ,
various years.

   *   Preliminary

  **   In 1978, Saudi Arabia contributed 30,862,000 JD to
the Central Government's foreign receipts.

economic fortunes of its friends. Thus, up to the late 1950s, Britain provided virtually all these funds. When these rapidly dried up with the
dismissal of Glubb Pasha (see Chapter 5), the United States stepped in to
fill the void. After the 1967 war, the Arab countries became almost the
sole donors, but Arab contributions declined radically after the 1970 civil
war, with the United States making up most of the difference. In the
post-1973 period, the wealth of Jordan's Arab neighbors began to play a
role that has rapidly increased as the United States's role has declined in
both absolute and relative terms.

Table 4.5:   Government Finances

(In Million J.D.)

	1975	1977	1979*
Total Revenues	199.4	323.0	447.1
Domestic	82.6	142.2	180.9
Taxes on Income	(4.3)	(16.0)	(25.9)
Taxes on Imports	(20.9)	(64.0)	(71.2)
Grants & Technical			
Assistance	100.6	122.2	203.2
Foreign Borrowing	16.2	58.5	63.0
Total Expenditures	204.9	337.8	495.6
Recurring	125.7	195.6	291.5
Capital	79.2	142.3	204.1
Government Domestic			
Borrowing Requirement	+5.5	+14.9	+48.5
Internal Public Debt	65.4	109.8	150.4
External Public Debt	107.8	193.1	244.4**

Source: Central Bank of Jordan,   Monthly Statistical Bulletin,
          various years.

Note: Discrepancies in totals due to rounding.

   *   Preliminary

  **   1978

GOVERNMENT FINANCE

Domestic participation in the revenues and expenditures of the Jordan government is markedly low. In 1979, the most recent year for which data are available, domestic revenues were only 37 percent of total expenditures; direct taxes, or income tax, were only a minuscule 5 percent of expenditures (see Table 4.5). If only recurring costs are considered – that is, excluding capital costs, which are heavily inflated by Jordan's large development efforts – still the domestic participation is only 62 percent of these costs. This extreme imbalance is made up by the largess of Jordan's friends in the Arab world and the West. And this overall pattern has remained relatively constant since the 1950s.[3] This situation over a period of time creates a dependency syndrome as well as a need constantly to seek out nondomestic sources of government funding that necessarily affects Jordan's foreign policy and behavior vis-à-vis its financial friends. The manner in which this problem is to be addressed is discussed in the next section.

GOVERNMENT PLANNING FOR DEVELOPMENT

Jordan has been frequently described as "plan happy." Seemingly, the government is constantly involved in drawing up plans and studies to back up various segments of the comprehensive multiyear plans. Nonetheless, Jordan's multiyear plans, although by no means entirely realized, have been of significant help in the development process. First, they have lent direction, coherence, and emphasis to the overall effort. Second, they sketch out specific designs for planned growth in GDP, personal income, and trade, which in turn are benchmarks against which progress may be measured. Third, explicit major and many minor projects are listed in detail. This planning exercise is not only a description of what is to be done, but also provides a major document for development fund-raising purposes, that is, the document may be (and is) used as a sophisticated shopping list.

In 1981 Jordan embarked on its fifth plan. The first was a general five-year plan covering the 1962–1967 period. It was scrapped in 1964 and replaced by a seven-year plan that gave much more detail about specific projects and was thus more usable as a means to attract financing. It also provided a blueprint for Jordan's capital investment intentions for the subsequent seven years. With the onslaught of regional and domestic nation-threatening events, planning was virtually forgotten in the 1967–1972 period. In 1972, an interim three-year plan was published, marking Jordan's return to normalcy. The five-year plan of 1976–1980 was considerably more significant, including as it did growth projections for all sectors as well as a listing of numerous projects in these sectors.

When it was published, the five-year plan of 1976 was to some extent ridiculed, but Jordan largely proved its critics wrong. The latter specifically focused on what they claimed were excessive projections for growth of the whole economy and of the specific sectors. In addition, the shopping-list nature of the plan was derided, but in the subsequent years Jordan proved successful in attracting development finance capital for its plan. (See Tables 4.4 and 4.5 for gross figures on this.) According to spring 1979 information from the National Planning Council, the following results were achieved: (1) The projected annual growth rate of 12 percent had been met; (2) growth in social services was 19.6 percent versus the 16.5 percent anticipated in the plan; (3) a major reduction in the country's balance of payments deficit was not realized (this was ascribed to the four-year drought and the subsequent necessity of importing considerable grain and meat); (4) the real rate of annual growth in the agricultural sector was 5.5. percent versus the 7 percent projection in the plan; (5) industrial growth was 17.5 percent, the same as the plan's projections.[4]

The 1981–1985 development plan was publicly presented by the National Planning Council in spring 1981. Typically, the sectoral development projections were ambitious: (1) Agricultural income would grow 40 percent at an annual rate of 7 percent; (2) industrial and mining income would increase at a phenomenal 17 percent annual rate and would reach 29 percent of the total GDP by 1985; and (3) service-sector income growth would be slow, at 8.2 percent per annum. The plan includes a series of projects and programs, ranging from a focus on Jordan Valley development and livestock improvement to the potash mining and attendant industries, light manufacturing, and joint ventures with other Arab countries. Another important feature of the plan is the balancing of domestic government revenues with expenditures by 1985 by decreasing proportionately government expenditures and increasing domestic income through improved taxes and a stimulated economy. The population is expected to grow, realistically, at 5 percent per year, 3.8 percent on the basis of natural growth and 1.2 percent from migration from the West Bank and Gaza Strip. A set of goals, listed in sort of a potpourri form, included the following:

> Arab and other foreign investments are to be attracted through legal changes. Export-oriented industries will be promoted, emphasis will be put on manufacturing and complementary industries, the introduction of modern technology will be favoured and value added in industries using local raw materials will be increased, as will value added in agricultural production. Emphasis will be given to balanced regional development within Jordan. Local energy sources will be developed and water and energy conservation plans adopted.[5]

The institutions involved in the development process have grown over the years. Initially, development was in the hands of the Jordan Development Board, which was renamed the National Planning Council in the 1970s. The council is in charge of drawing up the master plan and then coordinating the government's role in its execution. For projects and data, it relies on the various ministries and specialized agencies. The latter are the Jordan Valley Development Authority, which is in charge of the planning and execution of the major development program in the northern and southern Jordan Valley and all the tributaries leading to it, and the Royal Scientific Society, which is a kind of "think tank" designed to take a more studied look at development-related problems, ranging from the role to be played by different sectors of the economy to the investigation of solar energy technology. Finally, in keeping with the Hashemites' strong emphasis on development, since the beginning of the 1970s Crown Prince Hassan, the king's brother, has taken direct charge of the effort. He is very much in evidence in the popular promotion of economic and social development, but he is also deeply involved in the substance of planning. In this role, he is chairman of the National Planning Council and the Royal Scientific Society.

Major planning exercises necessarily raise the question of excessive control from the center – which is highly probable – versus the desire for more regional and local input and authority – and Jordan is no exception. Government personnel of all categories are involved in the planning effort: employees of the National Planning Council, functionaries in the ministries, and even local governors. While they definitely profess the general ideal that the local population should be involved in planning, in actuality they are very development-oriented, are tied to the overall plans, and are judged by their superiors by the degree of implementation of the relevant aspects of those plans. This leads to the syndrome of imposing many development activities from the center and from above. On the other hand, as more and more economic resources become available, the local people increasingly wish to gain some measure of authority over them, whether it is through a cooperative, municipality, a community-based society, or the like. A reverse image of the local people's concern is the perception of some top policymakers that the government gives excessively to the people and the people give very little in return. Pointed to as partial evidence is that a very small proportion of government revenues or expenditures is derived from the people and that the government, especially since the mid-1970s, is the source of increasing largess. Parenthetically, it should be noted that this criticism is somewhat in contradiction to reality: Local communities usually contribute 50–60 percent of the costs of village-level projects.

In recent years, leading policymakers have begun to address these problems. In response to the complaint that all decisions were made in Amman, Prime Minister Mudar Badran in the mid-1970s started holding cabinet meetings throughout the country to elicit regional and local input. At the end of 1979, King Hussein installed a new cabinet headed by the intelligent and perceptive Sharif Abdul Hamid Sharaf. Among the areas most stressed by Sharaf were "establishing direct, two-way communication between the governed and the governing through more public participation in the decision-making process," or in other words, "participation and decentralisation." In practical terms this would translate to "handing back real power to local governors, mayors and councils."[6] To implement these ideas, the government created a new mechanism, the regional councils, on which mayors, heads of village councils, and other appointed people sit. In theory, these councils are to have authority over policy concerned with the socioeconomic order, e.g., questions relating to housing, health, education, and the like. Also, and equally important, the council would provide a mechanism for power sharing. Inherent in this effort, in addition, was an attempt to address the problem of urban bias so that development could be spread more evenly throughout the country.

Due to his untimely death, Prime Minister Sharaf's government came to an end in mid-1980. The able Mudar Badran was soon to regain the prime ministership, and it is thought that a continued emphasis will be put on Sharaf's decentralization and power-sharing plans.

AGRICULTURE

The presence or lack of sufficient water (see Chapter 2) is the key to Jordanian agriculture. Taking this essential element as the variable, Jordan may be divided agriculturally into three parts: the highlands, which receive sufficient rainfall for cultivating grains and other crops not requiring significant quantities of water; irrigated areas, where citrus fruits and vegetables may be grown in quantity; and the desert margin, where animal husbandry is practiced but tilling the soil is usually not practicable, except for marginal catch crops. Only about 260,000 hectares (640,000 acres) of East Jordan's 9,000,000 (22,200,000 acres) are cultivated. The Ministry of Agriculture claims that 500,000 hectares (1,200,000 acres) are arable, but those not now tilled are marginal in the opinion of most experts. Of the 260,000 cultivated hectares (640,000 acres), 36,000 (89,000 acres) are irrigated, 22,000 (54,000 acres) of which are in the Jordan Valley.

Jordanian rainfall agriculture is typical of Middle Eastern dryland farming. The amount and distribution of rainfall varies considerably from year to year; there may be bountiful returns or returns not even equaling what the farmer planted. Where the average rainfall is lower, the fluctuation between sufficient rain and drought is even more radical. Wheat, which is grown on more than half the dryland area, gives an excellent example. In 1971/1972,[7] Irbid (a major wheat-growing region in the north) received about 450 millimeters (18 inches) of rain, and in 1972 Jordan harvested more than 200,000 tons of wheat. In 1972/1973, rainfall was 350 millimeters (14 inches) and the harvest was barely more than 50,000 tons. In 1973/1974 and 1974/1975 the figures were, respectively, well over 600 millimeters (24 inches) and 250,000 plus tons, and 340 millimeters (13 inches) and 50,000 tons. These figures demonstrate the volatility of rainfall and the correlation between rainfall and grain production. Thus, the farmer is yearly plagued by the problem of whether or not to plant.

Jordan is very far from self-sufficiency in wheat production, once again reflecting the problems of a population swollen by refugees. Indigenous production, on average, meets a little more than half the national requirement. Of the balance, about one-half is purchased and the rest is brought in free by the UNRWA for distribution to the refugees. This high dependency on external sources for the basic staple leaves Jordan quite vulnerable to food pressure. The government, however, has been somewhat schizophrenic with respect to encouraging wheat production. During the 1973–1976 period, Jordan essentially kept the market price of wheat below the world price, even though farmers had to pay world prices for all agricultural inputs. The reason for this policy seemingly was to control inflation. But by the late 1970s the government had reversed itself and was buying wheat from the farmers at prices above the international levels. Also, it started broadly pursuing methods of increasing production.

Introducing modern cultivation methods on the dryland farms has been somewhat problematic. The use of labor-saving devices such as tractors and combines is widespread; they are provided by both private entrepreneurs and agricultural cooperatives. Fertilizers, pesticides, and herbicides are also increasingly available and in use, again through both private and community-based cooperative channels. The introduction of the new grains developed in the Green Revolution, however, has been slow, because of two underlying problems. The new seeds require more water than average Jordanian rainfall provides, and they are soft wheat varieties rather than the hard wheat preferred by the people. New seeds of the hard wheat variety that require less water have been (and continue to be) developed, and in 1979 significant quantities were distributed through the cooperatives in the Irbid region.

The dryland area also produces barley, various animal forage crops, legumes, and a few vegetables. Fruit and nut trees as well as grapes are also grown widely. Olive trees are perhaps the major fruit-bearing tree, covering more than 30,000 hectares (74,000 acres); the combined area covered by other tree varieties is about 40,000 hectares (99,000 acres).

The status of agricultural labor was radically changed by the economic boom conditions in Jordan. Prior to the mid-1970s disguised rural unemployment and considerable underemployment were the norm. With the boom conditions, virtually all excess labor has moved to the cities, some marginal and even good land lies uncultivated, and numerous small uneconomical holdings are rented to others so that the

Table 4.6:   Landholding in Jordan

1975

Size of Holding in Dunums	Number of Holdings	Area in Dunums
- Less than 5	8522	16038.9
5 - Less than 10	3825	25679.2
10 - Less than 20	6929	92233.2
20 - Less than 30	5337	121850.5
30 - Less than 40	4666	150824.5
40 - Less than 50	2968	125914.4
50 - Less than 100	8634	570793.2
100 - Less than 200	5479	701828.7
200 - Less than 500	3359	933770.0
500 - Less than 1000	719	452125.3
1000 - Less than 2000	253	299725.5
2000 - Less than 5000	84	220487.5
5000 - Less than 10000	10	58520.0
10000 - Less than 25000	9	133800.0
- More than 25000	-	-
Total	50791	3904030.9

10 dunums equal 1 hectare

Source: Jordanian Department of Statistics, Agricultural Statistical
Yearbook and Agricultural Sample Survey, 1978 (Amman:
January 1979), p. xiii.

owner may take up another occupation and the renter may have sufficient land to cultivate.

Table 4.6 demonstrates the landholding pattern for all of Jordan.
Although some large holdings exist, the bulk are medium and small.
Also, 75 percent of the holdings, almost 75 percent of farmland, were
operated by the owner. Large holdings (200 hectares or more) were held
by a little more than a hundred people and constituted about 10 percent
of the farmland. More troublesome are the very small, uneconomical
holdings: Almost one-half are 3 hectares or less. The small holdings are
largely the result of the Muslim law on inheritance, which states that all
male offspring must inherit equally and all female children inherit one-
half of a male share. The uneconomical size of these plots is now being
partially overcome as holders who seek work in other sectors of the
economy rent their plots to others, a phenomenon that existed years ago
but increased dramatically in the 1970s.

The Jordan Valley is by far the most important irrigated area.[8]
Realizing that this valley was the only region in which agriculture could
be dramatically increased, the government has put considerable effort
and resources into it. In 1964, it completed the East Ghor Canal (al-Ghor

Irrigated agriculture in the Jordan Valley.

is the Arabic word for the Jordan Valley), an open conveyor from which farmers could draw water for their fields. Up until 1967, one hundred forty-five thousand people lived in and tilled the region, using relatively primitive techniques. The 1967 war and the subsequent guerrilla-related violence caused the population to decline radically to eight to ten thousand people, and the canal system fell into partial disuse. Once peace was reestablished, renewed emphasis was put on the Jordan Valley. The population again increased to eighty-eight thousand in 1979, and it is projected to reach one hundred fifty thousand in 1985. In the early 1960s and again in the early 1970s, 12,000 hectares (30,000 acres) were under cultivation. The cultivated area was increased to 22,000 hectares (54,000 acres) in 1976–1978 as the canal was lengthened and more water sources tapped. These sources were a series of small dams collecting water flowing from *wadis* and the more major King Talal Dam on the Zarqa River. An additional 14,000 hectares (35,000 acres) will be brought under cultivation if the long-planned Maqarin Dam is built on the Yarmouk River. However, despite the availability of funding from Arab countries, the U.S. Agency for International Development (USAID), and the World Bank, its construction could be thwarted by the sensitive issue of important riparian rights. These include the share of water not only for Jordan,

A bustling fruit market.

but also for Israel, for the West Bank (and its share relates to the future status of that territory), and for Syria.

Production in the Jordan Valley is primarily focused on truck garden vegetables and citrus trees and is very much designed for the export market. Due to the intensive use of irrigation, this valley, which constitutes only 0.6 percent of Jordan's land area, provides 90 percent of its export crops. This high level of productivity is being made possible by the modernization of the method of irrigation: The flood system is increasingly being replaced by sprinklers and drip networks with the attendant plastic hothouses when needed. The Jordan Valley Development Authority is also providing considerable infrastructure in the form of roads, electricity, potable water, schools, clinics, and some housing.

It is ironic that in a country once plagued by rural underemployment and unemployment, foreign laborers—more than twenty thousand Egyptians and Pakistanis—are now employed in the Jordan Valley. The Egyptians, it is reported, are unfortunately bringing their national debilitating disease, bilharzia (schistosomiasis), with them, but the government is actively attempting to prevent its spread. The valley is the only region subject to land redistribution; the law is designed to eliminate both very large and uneconomically small holdings, the upper and lower limits being respectively 20 hectares (50 acres) and 3–5 hectares (7.5–12.5 acres), depending on land quality. In actuality, by 1981 very little land had been redistributed under this formula.

Jordanian animal husbandry is based on both ancient and very modern methods. Red meat production, primarily sheep and goats, is in the hands of bedouin and settled people living along the marginal rainfall areas. Following a time-honored pattern, the sheep are moved to the desert or deep *wadis* when the fall rains come and the grass begins to grow. In the late spring, the rains and grass are gone and the sheep and goats are brought to the cultivated area, which has been harvested. Here the sheep feed on the stubble and specially provided animal fodder and use the local water sources. Farmers usually allow the animal herders to pasture the animals for free. The modern section is the highly efficient chicken houses or factories. The first stage of this industry was initiated in the West Bank; after 1967 some farmers restarted in the East Bank. By the mid-1970s, Jordan was self-sufficient in eggs and chickens, and when the Lebanese civil war severely curtailed Lebanese production and export, Jordanian farmers began their own export of chickens and chicks to the Arab oil-producing countries. It is estimated that all animal husbandry[9] and its products – meat, wool, leather, and dung – account for 45 percent of the gross value of agriculture, albeit the figures are subject to doubt.

A word needs to be added about agricultural cooperatives. The cooperative movement was officially introduced in Jordan in 1952. By 1954 there were fifty cooperatives, with 2,091 members, on both the West and East Banks. Slow but steady growth continued after this date, but with only limited capital input, and the functions of the cooperatives were limited largely to providing small agricultural loans (maximum of 100 JD). In the 1970s, the basic thrust was changed, partly to provide a mechanism for local decision making. The new thrust included the consolidation of small cooperatives into larger and presumably stronger multipurpose cooperatives. Additional capital was provided, and a full-time manager, usually an agronomist, was placed in each cooperative and paid by the Jordan Cooperative Organization, an autonomous government agency. By 1978 the movement included 11,500 members in 139 agricultural multipurpose cooperatives with a paid capital of 580,000 JD and 328,000 JD in reserves. Benefiting from experts provided by the Ministry of Agriculture, the cooperatives operate in the following areas: seasonal and medium-term credit, provision of agricultural supplies and technical services, and ownership and operation of agricultural machinery. With the exception of sheep and goat herders, from one-quarter to one-half of all farmers are members of and benefit from these multipurpose cooperatives.[10]

INDUSTRY AND MINING

Since 1950, the industrial sector's share of Jordan's GDP advanced from virtually nil to almost 20 percent. And this remarkable growth was strongly in the private sector, although the government provided essential support and often equity participation. The early emphasis was on both mineral extraction for export and industry for import substitution. These trends have certainly continued, but added to them are significant industry for export and a recent emphasis on the establishment of larger-scale and technologically more sophisticated industries.

The government's promotion of the industrial sector may be divided into five categories. First, as noted previously, the government continues to create the physical infrastructure on which industry may grow. This involves roads, transportation, and supply of electricity and water. Second, government equity investment in companies is quite common, especially in the larger corporations that require considerable capital. Such participation may range from 10 to 20 percent or up to 93 percent, as in the Jordan Phosphate Mines Company Ltd. Third, in the 1970s Jordan put on the books the Encouragement of Investment Law, which, inter alia, includes for newly established industries an income and social service tax exemption for up to nine years, customs exemption on equipment, and guaranteed repatriation of capital and free transfer of profits. At the same time, industrial free zones were created at Aqaba, Zarqa, and at the Jordan-Syria border. Fourth, the government generally provides a high level of protection against import competition and protects established industries from the entry of new firms while encouraging the latter to go into new or other fields. Fifth, the government undertakes large-scale surveys for potential mineral extraction, and it occasionally conducts feasibility studies for potential new industries or mining ventures.

The leaders in Jordanian industry are five, two of which are extractive—phosphates and potash—and three of which are processing—petroleum products, fertilizers, and cement. The last two use locally produced natural resources. Of these, phosphates are critical to the economy, providing 57 percent of commodity exports and generating funds for the government's development plans. Table 4.7 indicates that this industry more than doubled production in the 1975–1979 period. Capacity in 1979 was almost 3,000,000 tons, and the plan is to increase it to 7,000,000 tons by the mid-1980s. Potash production is only just starting, with the expectation that 1,200,000 tons will be produced in 1982. The industry is located on the Dead Sea, from which the Israelis initiated production in the 1950s. Fertilizer production, based on Jordan's phosphate,

Table 4.7:   Industrial Products of Principal Industries

Principal Industries		Production	
	Unit	1975	1979
Phosphates (dry)	000 Tons	1352.2	2828.1
Cement	000 Tons	572.2	623.2
Petroleum Products	000 Tons	828.2	1612.4
Electricity	mill. KWH	374.4	774.1
Iron & Steel	Tons	31304.0	80961.0
Textiles	000 yards	952.6	1416.7
Pharmaceuticals			
Liquid	000 Liters	358.9	607.0
Other	000 Tons	113.4	158.1
Cigarettes	mill. cig.	1846.0	3414.1
Paper	Tons	4190.0	7123.4
Leather			
Sole	Tons	531.4	190.7
Upper	000 sq. ft.	2215.4	2448.9
Spirits	000 Liters	5502.0	7206.7
Liquid Batteries	000 Batts	44.4	62.9
Detergents	Tons	4202.6	10567.3

Source: Central Bank of Jordan, Monthly Statistical Bulletin, various issues.

started in 1982 in what will, when it is completed, be Jordan's second largest industrial plant. Cement has long been produced in Jordan, again based on local minerals. Capacity was sufficient for local demand until the economic boom of the 1970s, which virtually doubled demand and resulted in considerable importation. In order to meet this new demand level, capacity is rapidly being increased; it was slated to reach 1,200,000 tons per year in 1983. Finally, petroleum products are refined from Saudi Arabian oil pumped to Jordan. Capacity, which almost doubled from 1975 to 1979, is to be doubled again by 1981, bringing capacity to 3,800,000 tons.

Industries smaller than the big five include pharmaceuticals, iron and steel, ceramic tiles, textiles, cigarettes, paper, shoes (leather and plastic), paints, detergents, and wet batteries. Many experience an annual turnover in the range of $5,000,000 to $25,000,000. And they are both import-substitution and export-oriented industries.

A final note needs to be made about the construction and services sectors of the economy. They too experienced considerable growth,

Workers in a pharmaceutical plant.

especially in the 1970s, but suffered considerably in the 1967–1971 period when tourism was nonexistent and construction very slow. For example, in 1967 and again in 1971, construction in Amman and Zarqa dipped below 50,000 square meters (60,000 square yards) of space, but in 1976, 1977, and 1978 it sustained itself at more than 400,000 square meters (478,000 square yards) per year. Tourism, which affects businesses as diverse as transportation, hotels, handicrafts, and restaurants, has seen significant growth – there were fewer than one hundred fifty thousand visitors in 1960 and more than a million by 1980. Westerners come to tour Jordan's ancient and beautiful sites, such as Jerash, a Roman trading town, or Petra, the Nabatean capital carved out of the sides of pink sandstone mountains. Three-quarters of the tourists are Arab, coming to enjoy a mild climate and a relatively free life. As noted above, Arab tourism increased significantly with the demise of Lebanese tourism due to the seemingly never-ending conflict in that unfortunate country.

A Roman amphitheater in the center of Jordan's capital, Amman.

NOTES

1. Unless otherwise cited, the data in this chapter are derived from Jordanian publications and/or conversations with Jordanian government officials.

2. Actually in 1979 and 1980, the governor of the Central Bank of Jordan reported that there was a surplus of 64 million JD and 30 to 50 million JD respectively (private communication from Rami G. Khouri, a Jordanian reporter).

3. Michael P. Mazur, *Economic Growth and Development in Jordan* (Boulder, Colo.: Westview Press, 1979), p. 125. Mazur also noted that the revenue and expenditure data are not entirely reliable. Many observers believe that significant amounts of military aid are not included in the published figures.

4. Interviews at the National Planning Council, spring 1979.

5. Jenab Tutunji, "Industry Favoured in New Five-Year Plan," *Middle East Economic Digest* (London), March 27, 1981, p. 20.

6. Rami G. Khouri, "New Broom in Jordan," *Middle East International* (London), February 15, 1980, p. 7.

7. The rains last from mid-fall to mid-spring, and the wheat harvest is in late spring and early summer. (All tons are metric tons.)

8. Most of this material comes from interviews with officials of the Jordan Valley Development Authority.

9. Ministry of Agriculture data for 1978 indicate there were 856,000 sheep and goats, 6,000 cows, 1,623,000 laying chickens, and 22,090,000 broiling chickens.

10. Jordan Co-operative Organization, "The Co-operative Movement in Jordan," Amman, September 1979, pp. 5, 16–17.

5

History

The area of modern Jordan was involved in most of the major historical movements in the Middle East owing to its central position, bordering on, or lying close to, Egypt, Palestine, Syria, and Arabia. Human habitation in the area can be dated back to 6000 B.C. through various monuments and drawings. The area first appeared in recorded history in 2400 B.C., during the Bronze Age, with an advanced sedentary agricultural civilization, but this suddenly and inexplicably disappeared in 1800 B.C. The thirteenth century B.C., during the Iron Age, witnessed the rebirth and resettlement of East Jordan by four Semitic peoples—the Edomites, Moabites, Ammonites, and Amorites, who covered the area from the south to the north. Their economies were agriculturally based, but with a trading overlay, and each group maintained its portion of the famed King's Highway that stretched from Aqaba through Shawbak, Tafila, Karak, and Madaba to Damascus. During the tenth century B.C., the Israelites, led by the great kings David and Solomon, conquered and ruled the area, but the Moabites gained strength and under their great king Mesha, around 850 B.C., regained control of Jordan from Aqaba to Madaba. For the next two hundred fifty years, these various groups vied for position, and during the sixth century B.C. the area generally collapsed economically, reverting to a more sparsely settled pastoral economy with very little central order.

Alexander the Great of Macedonia brought the area its first direct contact with European culture, a mutual interchange that would continue, albeit with occasional breaks, during the next two millenia. During his short reign (330–323 B.C.) and those of his successors, Seleukus and the Ptolemies, the region prospered. Hellenic culture was encouraged, cities were built, and the region became important to trade routes in the area.

Preceding Alexander the Great by one hundred fifty to two hundred years were the Nabateans, who controlled the area from Karak to the Red Sea, which had formerly been under Moabite rule. The Naba-

73

teans, an Arabic-speaking people, were famous as traders as well as for their unique capital carved out of the rose-colored walls of Petra. Alexander and the Ptolemies never conquered the Nabateans, but the Hellenic cultural influence on their architecture became quite pronounced. The Romans had more success. By 70–60 B.C., they controlled the northern part of Jordan, including the cities built during the Hellenic period. And the Nabatean area, although flourishing in trade, agriculture, and culture, came to be a vassal state to Rome. In A.D. 105, the Romans imposed direct rule, built a series of forts to control the desert, and often resorted to payments to bedouin tribes – a practice continued to the current century – to protect the trade routes. By the early third century, the Nabateans had declined as trade shifted from Petra to Basra at the northern end of the Arabian Gulf. And another Arab tribe, the Ghassanids, arrived in the region and displaced the Nabateans, ending their eight-hundred-year presence.

In A.D. 330 the Roman Empire's capital shifted to Byzantium (Constantinople); the empire eventually came to be known as the Byzantine Empire. Emperor Constantine (324–337) converted to Christianity, and most of the people of Asia Minor and the Levant followed suit. The Ghassanids, who became Christian during this period, were an important part of this Byzantium complex. Their leader, Harith ibn Jahal (529–569) was even named the king of the Arabs by Emperor Justinian. During Harith's reign and the following hundred years, the empire was seriously weakened by constant fighting with the Persians and by internal decay.

The early seventh century witnessed a fundamental change in the region that influences Jordan and its neighbors to this day – the arrival of Islam, a newly developed religion with strong roots in Christianity and Judaism. Between 629 and 636 Arab Muslims coming from Arabia conquered the disintegrating Byzantine Empire. The key battles of Mu'ta and Yarmouk were fought in or near present-day Jordan. Then ensued a succession of dynasties: the Umayyads, based in Damascus; the Abbasids, with their capital in Baghdad; the Fatimids of Egypt; and the Seljuk Turks of the East. Throughout this period, Jordan was something of a backwater, known primarily for its position on the route to Mecca. In the twelfth century, parts of Jordan fell to the Crusaders, the center of their control being in Karak, where they built a magnificent castle fortress. In 1187, however, they too were defeated by Salah al-Din (Saladin), who initiated the Ayyubid dynasty. This dynasty lasted a hundred years and was replaced by the Mamluks, who ruled from Damascus for three hundred years.

The Ottomans, having built up their empire in Asia Minor and Europe over a couple of centuries, finally turned their active attention to

The Treasury of Petra, cut into the side of a pink sandstone mountain.

Roman forum in the ancient city of Jerash. Roman amphitheater in the foreground.

the Arab world and easily defeated the Mamluks in 1518, gaining control of much of the Arab Middle East, including Jordan. For the greater part of the Ottoman presence in Jordan, which lasted until 1918, little control was exercised. Rather, the authorities sent occasional military patrols through the area, rarely collected taxes, and paid bedouin tribes to safeguard the pilgrimage route. Actual control was left in the hands of small tribes, which tilled the highlands where sufficient rain falls, and the larger tribes of the marginal land, which practiced animal husbandry. This pattern was broken in the nineteenth century when the Egyptian army under Ibrahim Pasha, son of the Egyptian khedive Muhammad Ali, conquered and controlled the Levant from 1831 to

1841, and again in the late 1860s and 1870s, when the Ottomans started to assert direct control in the northern part of Jordan. The latter was one aspect of a more general policy of regaining control over various outlying regions of the empire. At this time the Ottomans encouraged the Circassians to settle in the area. In 1893 the Ottomans took direct control of Karak and the southern portions of Jordan. This reassertion of control encountered little resistance, except in 1910 when the people of Karak led a violent but ill-fated revolt, as did the people of Hawran and Jabal Druze in southern Syria during the same year.

Largely because of the Ottoman direct interest in the area, the economy gradually improved, the people of the highlands started settling in villages, and from 1900 to 1908 the Hijaz railraod was constructed, both necessitating security and stimulating the economy.

But the Ottoman Empire collapsed at the end of World War I, and the Levant was eventually divided into mandates of Britain and France. The people of Jordan had fought on both sides during the war. On the one hand, most settled people and towndwellers sided with the Ottomans, some joining the regular army and others providing irregular horsemen for Ottoman battles against the bedouin.[1] On the other hand, the bedouin, especially the Huwaytat, provided the main fighters in Jordan for the Arab revolt against the Ottomans. This revolt, which was led in an overall sense by Sharif Hussein of Mecca (King Hussein's great-grandfather) and on the ground by one of his sons, Amir Faisal, was coordinated with the efforts of the British army and given a subsidy and some technical assistance by British officers.[2] During 1917 and 1918, the forces of both Sharif Hussein and the British general Allenby succeeded in conquering Palestine, East Jordan, and Syria.[3]

Following the breakup of the Ottoman Empire, the various factions continued their maneuvering and claims and counterclaims. The result was general instability, to say the least. Initially, the Levant was divided into three basic sectors: Palestine, under Britain; Syria (including East Jordan), under Amir Faisal; and Lebanon, under France. All three fell under the authority of General Allenby. The claim to Syria and Transjordan quickly came under dispute. In mid-1919, the last of the British forces were withdrawn from Damascus, leaving effective control to Amir Faisal, who in March 1920 was declared king by a congress of notables from Syria, East Jordan, and parts of Lebanon. France, however, objected to Amir Faisal's presence and control and, on the basis of agreements struck with Britain, succeeded in having the Allied powers at the April 1920 San Remo Conference officially assign it the mandate over Syria and Lebanon, but not East Jordan. Britain was assigned Palestine and Iraq. Following this international move, France drove King Faisal out of Damascus on July 25, 1920.

The international status of East Jordan then fell into limbo. From a local viewpoint, the situation basically reverted to the conditions of the mid-nineteenth century: little or no control from a central power. Limbo, however, was short-lived. In August 1920 the high commissioner of Palestine, Sir Herbert Samuel, went to Salt and declared that, with the fall of King Faisal, East Jordan came under British mandate and that he would send a few political officers but would not administer East Jordan directly.

Shortly, Amir Abdullah (brother of Faisal and grandfather of King Hussein) arrived on the scene. In the fall of 1920, with a group of armed supporters, he stopped in Maʿan, which, at the time, was not part of the British mandate but under Sharif Hussein of Mecca. There, he declared that he had come to put his brother back on the throne in Damascus. Although this call was not positively answered, he moved up to Karak, in the British mandate, in January 1921 and continued to tour the East Jordan towns during the winter. As Amir Abdullah was touring, the British were adjusting their policies to the new realities on the ground. To the ousted King Faisal, they offered the kingship of their Iraqi mandate, paying off one debt to the Hashemite family. As to East Jordan, they decided to offer it to Amir Abdullah, who was then present in the region, in exchange for his promise to renounce his claims on Syria. In a March 27, 1921, meeting with the then colonial secretary, Winston Churchill, Amir Abdullah accepted these conditions as well as a British subsidy and British mandatory presence.

The question of whether East Jordan was part of the Palestine mandate, legally or by intent, during this period is continually raised. Suffice it to say that the record is by no means clear, no argument has sufficient weight. However, it is clear from Sir Herbert Samuel's statement and from the mandate papers Britain submitted to the League of Nations that Britain did not intend to rule East Jordan (which came to be known as Transjordan) directly as it did Palestine (such a declaration does not imply that the opposite was previously true) and that Transjordan explicitly did not fall under the Balfour Declaration, the unilateral British document issued during World War I concerning the Jewish "national home" and Arab rights in Palestine.

AMIR ABDULLAH'S TRANSJORDAN

With Britain's acceptance of his stewardship of Transjordan, Amir Abdullah proceeded to establish his state. Three major themes become obvious in this effort: the attempt to maintain security, both internal and external; the creation of the trappings of a state, namely a parliament, government, and governmental functions; and the search for Arab unity.

Threats to security were to take three forms: bedouin raiding, tax revolts among sedentary people, and threats from across the southern border. Because the British head of the embryonic Arab Legion, Major F.G. Peake, perceived the bedouin to be the primary threat, he established a policy of recruiting from the sedentary population "to check the Bedouin and allow an Arab government to rule the country without fear or interference from tribal chiefs."[4] Whether by design or mistake, this policy led to recruitment from the very segment of the population that had neither supported the Arab revolt led by Abdullah's brother and father nor helped the British against the Ottomans—and it was directed against that segment of the population, namely the bedouin, who had been actively supportive of the Hashemites and the British. Peake's force was used to contain bedouin raiding, but significantly it also put down major revolts in the various towns. The revolts were largely against tax collection and the state's attempt to extend its rule outside the capital; the use of the Arab Legion and the British Royal Air Force in subduing the revolts went far in establishing the authority of the state.

The next stage was for Amir Abdullah's forces to protect the young state against outside encroachment. The Saudi incursion in 1922 under the leadership of King Abd al-Aziz ibn Saʿud provided the first opportunity, and a second, much larger attempted raid in 1924 provided the second. The latter produced a resounding victory for the Arab Legion and the Royal Air Force, demonstrating to the people the necessity of having these forces for their own security.

The second raid came in the middle of the final resolution of the status of Amir Abdullah's father, Sharif Hussein of Mecca. During World War I, Sharif Hussein had declared himself king of the Arab world. He most probably saw his sons as ruling over segments of his territory. In January 1924, he arrived in Amman and proceeded to conduct himself as if he were the ruler. At this time, the Turkish Grand National Assembly (the successor to the Ottoman government) abolished the caliphate, i.e., the Ottoman Empire's claim to lead all of Islam. Sharif Hussein promptly attempted to seize this opportunity and declare himself to be the new caliph. The Muslim world reacted very negatively to this declaration, as did the British when they saw the Muslim reaction. In March 1924, the British representative in Amman, Sir Alec Kirkbridle, finally succeeded, by a mixture of persuasion and coercion, in getting Sharif Hussein to leave Transjordan for Mecca, and subsequently the British cut off his subsidy. Ibn Saʿud took this opportunity to further his ambition of conquering all Arabia. In August 1924, he attacked Hijaz (in which Mecca is located) and Amman—two Hashemite bases. (It is presumed that he did not distinguish Hashemite Transjordan from Hashemite Hijaz. As noted above, the Amman attack was thwarted handily, but the Hijaz attack was partially successful. Consequently, in September, Sharif Hussein resigned in favor of another son, Amir Ali, who was eventually defeated by Ibn Sa'ud in 1925 as the latter consolidated what was to become Saudi Arabia. With then King Ali's defeat, the Transjordanian forces entered the Ma'an/Aqaba area, claiming it had long been part of Transjordan. This territorial division was recognized by Saudi Arabia over the next five years.

With major external threats finally settled, the authorities turned to the more mundane instability caused by bedouin raiding. In 1926–1927, the Palestine mandate authorities created the Transjordan Frontier Force, recruited from Palestine, to guard the frontiers and attempt to stop cross-border raiding. The Arab Legion was to handle internal raiding, which continued to grow until it became an acute problem. To address this, Major J. B. Glubb was assigned to the Arab Legion in 1930. Reversing Peake's policy, he promptly recruited bedouin into the Arab Legion, precisely to patrol the bedouin region. His philosophy, unlike Peake's, was that the bedouin should be included in the state if the state wished them to "behave," and recruiting them into the army realized this goal. The legacy of this new policy has been felt throughout the history of Jordan as the bedouin became strongly loyal supporters and defenders of the Hashemite regime in the country. And by 1932, bedouin raiding had ceased.

Amir Abdullah moved sedately in building up other aspects of the state structure. Perhaps the most important institution was the amir's broad contacts with the people of Transjordan. To assure accessibility, throughout his life he opened his palace on Fridays to those who wished to discuss issues or register complaints. Amir Abdullah carefully cultivated leading families in both the sedentary and bedouin tribes. In a country of a few people, the amir could effectively reach large segments of the total population.

Structurally, Amir Abdullah ruled through an executive council drawn from notables of Transjordan as well as expatriates from Hijaz and Palestine. A British resident as well as various technical advisers were in place, at times dominating certain decisions. The question of some form of parliament was constantly raised. During 1923–1924, under the authority of Amir Abdullah, a basic law of elections was drafted, but the British resident caused it to be abandoned in favor of a much weaker legislative council that would approve executive council decisions. And in 1928, the Anglo-Jordanian Treaty, with the attendant Organic Law, was signed. This law, which included provisions for an in-directly elected representative body with weak powers, it is reported, was essentially imposed on Amir Abdullah; true negotiations were not honored.[5]

Amir Abdullah (center) with Health Minister Dr. Jamil Tutunji (left) and other officials in the late 1930s.

Opposition to the lack of representation and British oversight did not come from the bedouin or even the sedentary people in the villages, but rather from a small group of nationalists and antiregime elements in the urban areas. They provided the popular pressure for a parliament in the 1920s and were part of the 1926 Assembly of Notables delegated to write an electoral law. In the late 1920s they held a series of meetings called National Conferences, advocating elected representation, opposing the British presence, and pushing for liberal reform. Actually, the first Legislative Council under the 1928 law carried on in the same tradition and was critical of the authorities. When it refused to pass a bill funding part of the army, Amir Abdullah dissolved it. These actions were harbingers of the quite troubled relationship the Jordanian Hashemite monarchs have had with elected institutions. Future councils contained a different set of men who were more compliant. Nationalists like Kamel Abu Jaber, writing in the 1960s, were very critical of the British – and indirectly Amir Abdullah – for not allowing a more democratic tradition to emerge.[6]

Other aspects of the state also emerged slowly. The amir inherited the Ottoman tax system, which he applied until a cadastral survey was carried out, allowing for a new land-based tax system to emerge. Additionally, health and educational services developed much more slowly than did the security forces. Seemingly the mandatory power was more interested in applying its subsidy to the latter than the former. Once independence was realized in the late 1940s, this trend was reversed and these services were rapidly developed (see Chapter 3).

The onset of World War II brought a quickening in the pace of Transjordanian history. Shortly after the start of the conflict in Europe, the amirate declared war on Germany, even though most people thought this would have little meaning because there was at that time no Middle East theater of the war. This situation quickly changed in 1941. In Iraq, Rashid Ali and a number of generals conducted a pro-Axis coup d'etat, and in Syria, the Vichy French took over. Britain led attacks against both, and Transjordan's Arab Legion saw limited fighting in support of British troops in both countries. Although Amir Abdullah continually pushed for further active involvement of the Arab Legion in the Allied effort, Britain did not find a suitable theater for this to occur. The Arab Legion did serve guard duty in Palestine, relieving British troops for other fronts. It should also be noted that Amir Abdullah's commitment of troops and strong public statements in support of the Allies in 1940 were decidedly against the current trend in the Arab Middle East, where many were predicting Axis victory and actively seeking contacts with the Axis or its sympathizers.

Following World War II, Transjordan became the "independent" Hashemite kingdom of Jordan. On March 22, 1946, Transjordan and Britain signed a new treaty that laid the basis for this change, and on May 25, 1946, Amir Abdullah officially became king of Jordan. During this period Jordan promulgated a new constitution to replace the 1928 Organic Law that had been operative to that date.

But was Jordan truly independent? The terms of the treaty were somewhat restrictive and did not reflect an agreement between equals, as was claimed. Clauses of the treaty included British rights to maintain bases and station troops in Jordan, British transit rights through Jordan, and the continuation of heavy British involvement in – that is, virtual control of – the Arab Legion through the presence of British officers in command positions and a sustained British subsidy for its maintenance. Given these terms, Jordan's neighbors, Syria and Lebanon, were highly critical of the treaty, contending that it just recognized British occupation. Jordan's application for membership in the United Nations, although strongly supported by Britain, was de facto rejected by the Soviet Union and was not actively supported by other UN members because of the qualifications to the country's independence. In addition, the United States, among other nations, declined to recognize the "independent" state at that time.

In March 1948, Britain and Jordan renegotiated the 1946 treaty. The new terms were somewhat milder but still restrictive with respect to independence. The motivation for the new treaty was twofold: (1) The expiration of Britain's Palestine mandate was just two months away, and Britain wanted to regularize in a more acceptable format its relations with Jordan before the anticipated troubles erupted in Palestine; and (2) the British foreign secretary, Ernest Bevin, wished to negotiate a series of treaties with Middle Eastern countries to implement his plan for an over-all Middle Eastern alliance under Britain's auspices. As it turned out, Iraq rejected a draft treaty submitted to its government, Saudi Arabia broke off negotiations, and negotiations were never initiated with Syria and Lebanon.

A third major theme which ran throughout the history of the amirate and the first years of the kingdom was Amir Abdullah's constantly reiterated goal of unity for the Arabs. In essence, the notion of Arab nationalism and thus Arab unity dates back to the nineteenth century, when small groups began thinking and writing about the concept. Sharif Hussein, Abdullah's father, very much took up the cause during World War I, hoping to be king of the Arab Middle East. Amir Abdullah envisioned himself as being heavily involved in this movement, and it will be recalled that he entered East Jordan supposedly to put King Faisal back on the throne in Damascus. Consequently, the amir, erratically at first but in a more sustained manner later, promoted Arab unity, usually in a Greater Syria mode – that is, he always contended that Transjordan was a southern part of Syria and that ideally the various parts of Syria should be joined.

Arab reaction varied. In the interwar period, traditional Syrian leaders were split. Some endorsed the amir's call; others argued that Transjordan was solely a southern appendage of Syria and should be absorbed, with little or no role for Amir Abdullah. Iraqi leaders mirrored Syria's positions until the death of Amir Abdullah's brother King Faisal in September 1933, after which Amir Abdullah increasingly spoke of Syrian-Iraqi unity, with himself as king. In Palestine, the traditional split between the Hussaini and Nashashibi notable families was echoed in their positions, with the former strongly opposed to Amir Abdullah's self-projected role in Arab unity plans (as well as being opposed to him on most matters) and the latter in support of the amir. In Saudi Arabia, King Abdul Aziz strongly condemned the amir's plan, undoubtedly objecting to the expansion of Hashemite authority.

During World War II, the tempo of Arab unity plans picked up. Amir Abdullah both directly and through his Legislative Council pressured Britain and Syria on his Greater Syria concept. These calls for unity were repeated in 1941, 1942, and 1944. Britain's reply was that it would go along only if the other Arab countries agreed.

A rival trend started in 1942 when Nuri al-Said of Iraq and Nahas

Pasha of Egypt started pushing for Arab union. Clearly, Iraq and Egypt are decidedly superior in population, size, and strength to Transjordan. Britain was more responsive to their desires, and the push for Arab unity fell into their hands. Their efforts, with the blessing of Britain, resulted in the signing of the Alexandria Protocol for the formation of the League of Arab States. Signatories were Egypt, Iraq, Lebanon, Syria, and Transjordan on September 25, 1944, and Saudia Arabia and Yemen signed within six months.

This defeat did not deter Amir Abdullah. He brought up the Greater Syria plan as an Arab League agenda item in 1947 and made it a central part of his speeches from the throne in 1946 and again in 1947. His persistence brought strong reaction: Egypt and Saudi Arabia submitted sharply worded objections on behalf of Syria to then King Abdullah. But as the 1947 UN resolution to partition Palestine into Arab and Jewish states was passed over the objection of the Arabs, King Abdullah changed his focus, claiming the Greater Syria plan was the sole solution to the Palestine problem.

ISRAEL'S CREATION AND JORDAN'S EXPANSION

The November 29, 1947, UN General Assembly resolution, supported by the United States and the Soviet Union, was to be the internationally blessed catalyst for change in Palestine, Jordan, and the entire Middle East. The Arab States objected to the partition and establishment of a Jewish state on what they regarded to be Arab land. But Britain, feeling unable to resolve the issue, went ahead and announced that the mandate would be terminated on May 14, 1948.

Britain and Jordan, within the context of the new and changing reality, proceeded to make plans for the next stage. During the negotiations for the new British-Jordanian treaty of 1948, which were attended by Prime Minister Tawfiq Abdul-Huda and Brigadier John B. Glubb for Jordan and Foreign Secretary Bevin for Britain, it was apparently agreed that Jordan's Arab Legion would occupy those areas of Palestine allotted to an Arab state under the UN resolution. Brigadier Glubb further limited the legion's area of occupation to the West Bank region because he judged that the Arab Legion was too small to take over the Gaza Strip and Galilee as well. Bevin's response to the proposal was: "It seems the obvious thing to do, but do not go and invade the areas allotted to the Jews."[7] In addition, arrangements were made for Britain to release those sections of the Arab Legion in service in Palestine to Jordan so that they could participate in whatever action was necessary.

On the cessation of the mandate on May 14, 1948, the establishment of the state of Israel was declared, and the following day Jordanian troops entered what was to become the West Bank as well as a large salient stretching to Lydda-Ramle, which had also been assigned to the Arabs in the 1947 UN resolution. Egyptian troops entered southern Palestine, and Iraqi, Syrian, and a few Lebanese troops advanced in the north. With the exception of the Arab Legion, the Arab troops were ill-trained and ill-equipped, and they were shortly defeated by Israeli soldiers. The Arab Legion, too, was driven out of the Lydda-Ramle salient, the Israeli forces feeling that the force was too close to Tel Aviv and could block access to West Jerusalem. Glubb was roundly criticized for "allowing" the Israelis to occupy this area, and charges were made that he was taking orders from the British.[8]

During the spring of 1949, following the Egyptian negotiation of an armistice with Israel, Jordan negotiated a complementary one, but not without another major complication. Britain, desiring a common boundary between Jordan and Egypt, north of Aqaba and Eilat, introduced troops into southern Jordan in an attempt to back Jordan's control of such a frontier. Israeli troops, however, succeeded in reaching the Red Sea, securing a potential port at Eilat for the fledgling state. Faced with this reality and the fact that the land in question had been allotted to the Jewish state in the 1947 UN resolution, Britain withdrew its pressure for a Jordanian-Egyptian common border.

The fate of the Palestinian territory held by the Arab forces at the termination of the war was at issue even before the fighting finally ceased. King Abdullah's forces were in military control of the West Bank and Egyptian forces retained the Gaza Strip; the other Arab armies had been forced out of Galilee. The jockeying for position centered on who would rule the West Bank. It was well known that King Abdullah wanted to include that territory in an expanded kingdom. All the Arab countries strongly objected. To counter King Abdullah's ambitions, an Arab government of Palestine was declared in Gaza in September 1948, under the leadership of Ahmad Hilmi Pasha and the mufti of Jerusalem, Haj Amin al-Hussaini, a long-time bitter foe of the king. All members of the League of Arab states, with the exception of Jordan, quickly recognized the "state."

On the other hand, several alternative steps were taken in quick succession with respect to the West Bank and the Palestinians who had fled to the East Bank. In October 1948 a Palestinian refugee conference of five thousand delegates was held in Amman, which inter alia rejected the Gaza Strip-based Palestine government and asked for King Abdullah's protection. In December, the very important Congress of Jericho was held. It drew the attendance of numerous West Bank notables, the latter being basically an alternative group to that led by Hilmi Pasha and Haj Amin al-Hussaini. The congress called for immediate union of the West Bank and Jordan, with Abdullah as king, and cabled this resolution to both the League of Arab States and the United Nations. The Jordanian parliament quickly approved the congress's resolution. In March 1949 the military government was replaced by civilian rule in the West Bank, and in May the king appointed a new cabinet that included Palestinians. In December the king laid down the final steps leading to West Bank annexation: (1) The separate administration for the territory was withdrawn and replaced by direct administration by Amman, and (2) the East Jordan parliament was dissolved by the king, and elections were slated for April 1950 for a parliament of twenty West Bankers and twenty East Bankers.

In harsh reaction to King Abdullah's bold moves, the various Arab countries, using quite strong language, attacked him in the press and on the radio for his "land grabbing." In the spring of 1950, his opponents suddenly had even greater ammunition when it was discovered that the king was conducting direct negotiations with Israel for a peace treaty. (Apparently, only a draft was completed, and this the king decided to reject for larger and more pressing political reasons.) The Arab press and radio exploded anew with bitter attacks and calls of treason. A move to expel Jordan from the League of Arab States ultimately failed when a majority of the Arab states decided such a move was too radical.

The consummation of the unity move came in spring 1950. Elections for the lower house of parliament were held on both the East and West banks in April; later King Abdullah appointed a house of notables, of which seven out of twenty were Palestinians. On April 24, both houses met and voted for the union of the West and the East banks under the kingship of Abdullah. The text of the resolution read:

> First its [parliament's] support for complete unity between the two sides of the Jordan and their union into one state, which is the Hashemite Kingdom of Jordan, at whose head reigns King Abdullah Ibn al Husain, on a basis of constitutional representative government and equality of the rights and duties of all citizens.
>
> Second, its reaffirmation of its intent to preserve the full Arab rights in Palestine, to defend those rights by all lawful means in the exercise of its natural rights but without prejudicing the final settlement of Palestine's just case within the sphere of national aspirations, inter-Arab cooperation and international justice.[9]

A most fascinating aspect to this resolution is the statement in the second clause that the kingdom's action and policy toward Palestine were taken "without prejudicing the final settlement of Palestine's just case within the sphere of national aspirations." This statement closely parallels King Hussein's policy today: He constantly reiterates the principle that the people of the occupied West Bank have the inalienable right of self-determination, a policy that allows for either independent statehood or some form of connection with King Hussein's Jordan (see Chapter 6).

In the aftermath of unity – which partially realized King Abdullah's Greater Syria ambitions – the government settled down to establish a new set of working relationships. Notable Palestinians from the West Bank were always included in the cabinet, especially those who had supported the king prior to 1948. The prime ministership continued to rotate among the three individuals who had dominated it since the 1930s: Samir Rifai,[10] Tawfiq Abdul-Huda, and Ibrahim Hashim. In East Jordan, King Abdullah continued his paternalistic rule, his close contacts with the settled tribes and the bedouin, and his constant and crucial cultivation of the Arab Legion. In the West Bank, he was building up a network to legitimize further his role there, but by no means did he eschew the strengthening of his security forces for ultimate political control. It should also be underlined that all West Bankers as well as all Palestinian refugees (that is, those Palestinians not from the West Bank) were given Jordanian citizenship. This was not the case in other Arab countries that found themselves with Palestinian refugees.

King Abdullah did have problems with parliament. Under the new constitution, the cabinet was responsible to the king, not to parliament, and parliament had little control over fiscal matters. Many members objected to this, as they did to the continuing British presence. The dissent became so strong that the king felt compelled to dismiss parliament in May 1951; he called for new elections in August.

King Abdullah was assassinated on July 20, 1951, however, before the elections were held. It was said that the assassin was part of a larger plot conducted by Palestinians concerned about the King's motives in the West Bank and especially about his secret negotiations with the Israelis. The assassination occurred on the steps of the most important mosque in Jerusalem, with the king's young grandson, then Prince Hussein, at his side. The symbols associated with the assassination have had a lasting effect on King Hussein and have helped to create his strong attachment to the West Bank and especially Jerusalem.

King Abdullah's oldest son, Prince Talal, was immediately crowned king. He had long suffered from mental illness, however, and was shortly removed from the throne by a vote of both houses of parliament on August 11, 1952. Prince Hussein was then declared king. At the time he was a minor, sixteen years old, necessitating rule by a regency council. When he reached the age of eighteen by the Muslim lunar calendar (seventeen and a few months by the Gregorian calendar) in May 1953, he took the constitutional oath as king.

The years 1948–1953 should be considered as a fundamental turning point in the history of Jordan. Many trends were coming to an end. Between the wars, the amirate of Transjordan had been pacified and consolidated. The bedouin had been brought into the national stream and developed loyalty to the Hashemites through their participation in the Arab Legion. Importantly, one regime had ruled the East Bank without interruption for three decades, and the people of the region were beginning to accept it as their government. Land was registered; values increased; and settled agriculture began to take on much more importance. But the paternal, almost shaykh-like, rule of Abdullah had come to an end. For example, under Abdullah, the old and young shaykhs of the amirate used to sit around his receiving room, kissed his hand, and cultivated a certain amount of respect for and rapport with him, but this relationship did not exist, and probably could not have existed, between the shaykhs and the young King Hussein. (As Hussein grew older and matured, this situation changed, however.)

Even before King Hussein's accession to the throne, many new trends had started. The West Bank and the refugees became part of the kingdom, adding new dimensions to the country. In a sense, it fell to the very young king and his advisors to recreate the nation. This process had begun even before 1953. The administration had expanded, not only to provide services for the enlarged kingdom but also to improve the quality and increase the quantity of these services. At the regional level, to the ever-present rivalries among the Arab states was added the growth of radical movements. Numerous coups d'etat took place in Syria, which affected Jordan, and in 1952 Gamel Abdal Nasser came to power in Egypt, a charismatic leader who would profoundly affect all the Middle East.

THE FIRST PHASE OF KING HUSSEIN'S REIGN: 1953–1966

The 1953–1966 period was marked initially by a series of nation-shaking crises but eventually evolved into what appeared to be a more peaceful, stable track. However, it was during this period that the seeds were sown for the literally state-splitting Arab-Israeli war of June 1967.

Jordan was a very different place in the 1950s from what it had been before 1948. The West Bank had been added, and more important, almost overnight the population came to be dominated by the Palestinians, a group of people with more sophistication, education, and wealth than the Jordanians of the East Bank. These fundamental alterations entailed not only basic economic and social changes, but they also substantially contributed to a rapid evolution of the political situation.

In essence, King Hussein attempted to continue his grandfather's policies. On the West Bank and among the Palestinians, he sought to eliminate the old leadership, which was opposed to the Hashemites, and to build up a new, alternative Palestinian leadership. As this process continued – not without considerable problems and setbacks – he maintained his reliance on steadfast East Bank support. Key cabinet posts were almost always in the hands of men known for their loyalty and often originating from rural tribal areas and certain loyal minorities. Finally, although the army was being rapidly expanded and Palestinians did join it, its backbone remained with the ever-loyal bedouin and tribal members from rural areas, who dominated the strike units. During the crises that marked the 1950s, these army units frequently were ordered into the streets to counter riotous mobs and restore order.

The conditions that promoted the crises of the 1950s were many. The most obvious was the addition of the Palestinians. On a political level, they bitterly faulted Great Britain for the loss of most of their homeland in Palestine. The Hashemites they considered to be lackeys of the British – or at least very friendly to them – and thus culpable. King Abdullah's negotiations with the new Israeli state for a peace treaty confirmed, for many Palestinians, the guilt and nonacceptability of the regime. The Palestinians did not easily accept – in fact strongly resented – the dominant role in the government and army of the East Jordanians, whom they viewed as less educated and less sophisticated. (As the differences between the two groups diminished and interconnections, including considerable intermarriage, increased, this source of resentment became less important.)

Despite their opposition to or even outright rejection of the Hashemite regime, Palestinians increasingly came to participate in the state system and thus, at least tacitly, to accept it. By virtue of its very existence, the power it possessed in the form of a loyal army, and the material benefits it controlled and disbursed, the state was able to assert its claim as the ruler of its territory and cause the people to interact with it. However, Jordan's hold or control over material benefits was somewhat undermined or called into question because the UNRWA managed and distributed many of these in the case of the officially registered Palestinian refugees.

A second set of conditions contributing to the crisis atmosphere was the strength of the Arab nationalist movement and the rise of Arab nationalist and Islamic political parties. Arab nationalism has been variously described as the overall predominant force that shapes the destiny of the Arab world and as a force or concept that is honored in the breach and not taken seriously by any Arab leader. Somewhere in between lies the actual situation, and even that alters as the years pass. At the very least, in a practical sense Arab nationalism provides a certain legitimacy to the involvement of Arab states, at various levels and in various sectors, in the affairs of other Arab states. Thus, Transjordan interfered in the affairs of its neighboring states when Amir and later King Abdullah promoted his Greater Syria plan. Equally, at the time, other countries, including Egypt, directly involved themselves in Jordanian politics and even attempted to keep King Abdullah from acquiring the West Bank.

In the 1950s, this outside Arab influence on Jordan took various forms. The best known in the West were the actions of President Gamel Abdal Nasser of Egypt. When Nasser came to power in 1952, Egypt was already one of the most important leaders of the Arab world, if not the paramount one. Once Nasser had consolidated his rule, and especially during and after the 1955–1956 period (the maneuverings over the Baghdad Pact and the Israeli-Franco-British invasion of Egypt), he developed a broadly effective charisma and leadership that dominated the politics of the Arab world until his death in 1970. He exerted this influence through the use of radio (the transistor was rapidly becoming widespread), and his people on the ground, namely the Egyptian embassies' staffs and agents, actively participated in the politics of other Arab countries by such means as influencing and buying politicians, organizing demonstrations and riots, and generally swaying opinions. In Jordan, such activities were especially strong in the 1954–1960 period. And all this Egyptian interference in Jordan – and other Arab countries – was in the name of Arab nationalism. Other Arab nations, especially Syria, Iraq, and Saudi Arabia, indulged in these practices but did not enjoy the influence Nasser did.

The second form of outside interference consisted of the pan-Arab and pan-Islamic parties. Those of any significance in Jordan were the Baʿth party, the Communist party, the Muslim Brotherhood, and the Islamic Party of Liberation, of which the first and third were the strongest.[11] All these parties were founded outside Jordan, and chapters, albeit all illegal (with the exception in certain instances of the Muslim Brotherhood), were founded in the country before King Hussein came to the throne. Although each had older leaders and various methods of organization and means for reaching the people, a common and important pattern was for teachers who had studied outside Jordan (no university existed in Jordan at the time) to bring the ideologies and idealism back with them and propagate them in the classroom.

Party membership in these extra-Jordanian, and usually anti-Hashemite, parties was broadly spread throughout the country, on both banks of the Jordan River. The poverty-stricken Palestinian refugees were as easy to recruit as were the more settled West Bank Palestinians, and East Jordanians were also converted to the pan-Arab or pan-Islamic revivalist causes, although to a lesser extent.[12] The only significant Jordanian group seemingly immune to the lure of these parties was the bedouin.

A third set of conditions contributing to crisis was the decline of British influence in the region, the rise of the U.S. role as British influence waned, and the growing Soviet influence. The role of these actors is detailed below.

A fourth condition was the existence of the new Israeli state and Jordan's relationship to it. Jordan's policy, realizing her inherent weakness vis-à-vis Israel, was, to avoid clashes and armed conflict. This was more easily decided than executed, however. The Israelis, sometimes spontaneously and sometimes in response to actions by Palestinian refugees undertaking raids or attempting to farm their former lands on the Israeli side of the border, undertook severe border raids against West Bank villages. The Arab Legion's inability to respond and its attempts to prevent Palestinians from crossing the border created increasing Palestinian bitterness toward it and the Hashemite regime. Basically this constant perceived or real Israeli threat and occasional use of military force served to destabilize the country, often at crucial times.

Aside from Israeli raids, the first major crisis King Hussein faced was the maneuverings around the Baghdad Pact, which Turkey, Iraq, and Iran signed with Britain in 1955. The United States took on only a subsidiary status within the pact because at the time it was courting Egypt and Saudi Arabia, which were adamantly opposed to the agreement. It was obvious, however, that the United States strongly supported the pact's aims, as it was designed to contain Soviet influence very much in the style of and in conformance to the policy of U.S. Secretary of State John Foster Dulles. Egypt and Syria, although their support was actively sought, were unalterably opposed to the treaty, which they saw as merely retying them to their former colonial masters and undermining Arab nationalism.

In these maneuverings, Jordan became the last battleground. High-level British and Turkish delegations visited Jordan in December 1955 and attempted to persuade the young king to adhere to the pact. Included in the inducements were very considerable financial aid for the army and defense guarantees. To counter this pressure, Egyptian General Abdal Hakim Amer, a close friend of Nasser and later commander of the Egyptian army, traveled to Jordan to argue against it. At the time, however, King Hussein seemed to accept the concept of the pact and, consequently, appointed a loyal new prime minister, Haza al-Majaly, to push it through. This effort was defeated in the streets, however. Radio propaganda, Egyptian agents, and political parties brought out the mobs, not only in the capital but also even in small towns of East Jordan. Although the bedouin army units were able to control the demonstrations, Haza al-Majaly resigned and Jordan declined to join the new defense pact.

In this atmosphere of very strong Arab nationalism, King Hussein was most vulnerable, both internally and externally, because of the continued presence of the British. Not only were British troops stationed on Jordanian soil under the auspices of the Anglo-Jordanian Treaty, but also the command of the Arab Legion was in British hands. The very fact of the British presence undermined the king, but perhaps more important, it had the potential of undermining the legitimacy of the Arab Legion as a national force—and one must remember that the legion was and is the ultimate protector of the Hashemite throne. As a result, King Hussein almost overnight dismissed General John Bagot Glubb as commander of the army in March 1956, and after a two-month interim appointment, placed his protégé General Ali Abu Nuwar in the post. Other British officers were replaced by Jordanians in the subsequent months to complete the process of Arabization. To complete the change, the name of the army was officially changed from the Arab Legion to the Jordanian Arab Army. Britain was officially offended by these moves but did not undertake to sever ties or other relationships, such as the annual subsidies, at the time.

Each of the next three years—1956, 1957, and 1958—was more momentous than the last. Government instability, chronic since 1954, continued unabated, with a rotation of prime ministers apparently unable to cope with the myriad of forces. In early 1956 an alliance of Egypt, Saudi Arabia, and Syria tried to pull Jordan into its orbit, away from the Hashemite-Iraqi connection. (Iraq still had a Hashemite on the throne in 1956.) Funding was offered, but integration of Jordan's military into a united command was required. Jordan countered by holding similar negotiations with Iraq. Iraq also brought troops up to its border with Jordan in response to Arab maneuvers but, more important, to respond to real and perceived threats from Israel, which escalated even higher when it was sugggested that the Iraqi forces would enter Jordan in force. To top it all off, President Nasser nationalized the Suez Canal, setting off an international crisis that was to culminate in the Israeli-Franco-British invasion of Egypt starting October 29, 1956. In this atmosphere, parliament was dissolved and new elections were called for October 21, 1956. The only other elections held under King Hussein's reign to that date had been in 1954, but by all accounts they were definitely not free, a condition that largely prevailed, except in the 1956 and 1962 elections.

The 1956 campaign and choice of candidates and political parties were dominated by the larger events and ideologies of the Middle East, and because of the freedom of choice in the elections, the results

Table 5.1:   1956 Parliamentary Election Winners

National Socialist	11
Communist	3
Ba'th	2
Arab Constitutional	4
Community	1
Muslim Brotherhood	4
Liberation	1
Independent	14
Total	40

Source: Derived from Naseer Aruri, "Jordan:
A Study in Political Development,
1923-65" (Ph.D. dissertation, Amherst:
University of Massachusetts, 1967),
p. 159

reflected them (see Table 5.1). The winner, the National Socialist party of Sulayman Nabulsi, was a Jordanian party with mass membership that, although it did not advocate the demise of the Hashemites, did oppose most policies put forth by the king. The Arab Constitutional and Community parties were virtually creatures of the regime and had only elite membership. Following traditional parliamentary practice, King Hussein requested Sulayman Nabulsi to form a government. Seeing the handwriting on the wall, the king also completed on October 25 a military agreement with Syria and Egypt that placed the three armed forces under the Egyptian commander, a move that finally put the Jordanian regime on one side of the Arab tug-of-war, with the Iraqi Hashemites isolated on the other side. Soon afterward, Nabulsi formed a government made up of the left-wing members of parliament, including a Communist, which promptly started taking positions challenging King Hussein on basic issues.

The Israeli-Franco-British invasion of Egypt in late October and early November once again changed the Middle East situation. The British invasion of a sister Arab country virtually demanded that Jordan break off treaty relations with Britain. The Nabulsi government promptly initiated negotiations for this purpose that were completed in late winter 1957. The Nabulsi government also struck an agreement with Egypt, Syria, and Saudi Arabia whereby they would replace the British subsidy (this never occurred in actuality) and requested the removal of Iraqi troops, which had earlier entered Jordan to protect the country against Israel. To cap this trend, Prime Minister Nabulsi was making statements questioning the very existence of the state – that Jordan could not live forever as a country and should be connected fundamentally with another Arab state.

King Hussein did not agree with this new direction. His initial objections were oblique, but by February and March he started to reassert his authority. His first moves centered on establishing a relationship with the United States, which, he hoped, would be an alternative powerful friend for his Hashemite throne and Jordan. The United States was also interested in such a relationship. Although critical of the Israeli-Franco-British invasion, the United States was more fearful of Soviet intentions and potential exploitation of the deteriorating situation. Consequently, on January 5, 1957, President Eisenhower issued the Eisenhower Doctrine, whereby the United States pledged to aid Middle Eastern countries against Soviet aggression and subversion. Although King Hussein did not formally approve this U.S. initiative, it provided a friendly umbrella under which he could operate. Of more immediate importance to the king was a source of funding to replace the British subsidy, which would soon come to an end. As noted, three Arab countries had promised to replace it, but King Hussein was not sanguine that this would ever occur. Consequently, he started negotiating with his new friends, the Americans, to make up the budgetary loss. When the Nabulsi government discovered the king's initiative, it objected, but King Hussein nevertheless succeeded in initiating a relationship with the United States that endures, despite ups and downs, to this day. Appropriately, in March the Anglo-Jordanian Treaty was terminated (all the British troops were out by fall) and the first U.S. aid started flowing during April.

A much greater immediate threat to the young king's throne was an attempted coup d'etat in the early days of April 1957.[13] This threat to the throne seemed to be from two, somewhat connected sources: the cabinet of Sulayman Nabulsi and a small but influential group in the Arab Legion. The first phase in this challenge to the king occurred on April 8 when an armored car regiment surrounded the capital, perhaps with the complicity of General Ali Abu Nuwar, commander of the army, but it was later dispersed by the Nabulsi cabinet when queried by the king. When the cabinet, however, attempted to shift key senior security people in its favor, King Hussein promptly dismissed it. Finding his close political friends unable to form a government, the king turned to General Ali Abu Nuwar, the leader of the secret military-based cabal, who put together a group headed by a former Nabulsi minister and a few independents. This action initiated the second phase of the threat to the throne. Thus while seemingly working at the political or cabinet level on behalf of King Hussein, General Abu Nuwar was actually attempting to move army strike units, bereft of their arms, into the desert and away from Amman. In the meantime, after the April 8 incident, King Hussein paid doubly close attention to his direct contacts in important army units. The military-based plot became known on April 13 when officers in Abu Nuwar's cabal ordered a key artillery brigade into the desert. It resisted and mutinied. In the tense atmosphere, rumors floated in the brigade that the king was dead. Back in the capital, a loyal officer gained access to the king and informed him of the developments. On hearing the officer's information, King Hussein immediately took Abu Nuwar and sped toward the large army camp in Zarqa, east of Amman. On the way, he met troops coming to Amman to aid him. In the ensuing minutes, the king was highly feted, and he had a difficult time saving Ali Abu Nuwar's life. At that point the attempted coup was over.

Even though there had been a major threat to the Hashemite regime, there was also a positive side. Because of his visibly courageous actions, King Hussein became the true leader of the army – and this only one year after he had dismissed General Glubb. The army's ultimate loyalty, despite a few unsympathetic officers and units, was proved in a tangible manner. Contributing strongly to the army's loyalty and the king's legitimacy within its ranks and among some civilian sectors were his earlier actions to Arabize the military. Thus – and this was very important in the larger arena of the Arab world – King Hussein no longer had to rely directly on foreigners to secure his throne from internal threats.

But this did not mean that Western aid was of little importance. To the contrary, the developing relationship with the United States helped the king to stabilize the situation in the wake of the thwarted coup when his erstwhile friends might have sought to interfere. During the rest of April, there were cabinet crises, demonstrations in numerous towns, and continued threats to the throne. In reaction, the United States declared that the independence and integrity of Jordan were vital to U.S. national interests and that it would assist Jordan, if necessary, on the basis of the Eisenhower Doctrine. In a show of force, the United States ordered the Sixth Fleet to the eastern Mediterranean. Additionally, it rapidly decided to aid the kingdom financially. Internally, the king's security forces carried out mass arrests, and the new loyal government totally banned the political parties and labor unions. It eventually forced the resignation of fifteen members of parliament opposed to the regime. At least temporarily, the situation was calmed.

The next major challenge came from the forces of Arab nationalism and the desire for Arab unity. These movements had gained exceptional strength in the aftermath of the 1956 Israeli-Franco-British invasion of Egypt and Egyptian President Nasser's subsequent and dramatic rise in popularity. The forces played a crucial role in Syria, which always considered itself to be central to the concept of Arab nationalism and unity. Due to this overall feeling and other numerous internal and external factors, Syria united with Egypt on February 1, 1958, to form the United Arab Republic. This being the first tangible act of unity in the Arab world, the atmosphere among the committed was euphoric and the pressure toward further unions was exceptionally strong. Many of Jordan's Palestinian citizens also viewed the Egyptian-Syrian union and potentially progressive Arab unity schemes generally as a means for them to regain their homeland, which by then had been under Israeli rule for ten years. In reaction to these substantive threats, on February 14 Jordan concluded a federation agreement with the Hashemites of Iraq, to which it had again drawn close in the second half of 1957. Admittedly this was solely an engagement of convenience to protect the small country in a time of great tension.

In neighboring Lebanon, civil war broke out in late spring 1958, with the forces of the opposition being supplied from Syria. On July 14, General Abdal Karim Qasim overthrew the Iraqi Hashemite throne, and in the aftermath one of Jordan's leading politicians was killed by Qasim's forces in Baghdad. Always fearful of Soviet advancement, the United States and Britain were worried that the revolutionary and Nasserite forces would play into the communists' hands. Equally, the internal situation in Jordan throughout the spring and summer constantly posed threats to the throne. Following the Iraqi coup, the United States and Britain decided to act to secure what they perceived to be the moderate forces in Lebanon and Jordan. The United States sent marines to Lebanon to separate the opposing factions. In Jordan, the United States flew in much-needed petroleum, and Britain sent in troops who, although they never saw action, were nevertheless a stabilizing force, important psychologically for the king. To control the streets, the king declared martial law and once again called on the loyal army. After a few months, this crisis passed and the British troops left.

During the following few years King Hussein gained much stronger control than he had previously enjoyed. Although smoldering opposition persisted, he largely contained it. The political parties were banned, and those leaders who persisted in pushing the various destabilizing causes were in prison. Parliamentary life also continued. The 1956 parliament was finally dissolved in 1961. The next parliamentary election (October 1961) was marked by a great lack of freedom: Most candidates had no opposition. The 1961 parliament was shortly dissolved, to be replaced by one elected in November 1962, but this time greater freedom of choice among competing candidates—even though without party affiliations—prevailed.

The relative calm in the post 1958-period could not remain for long.

The Egyptian-Syrian union broke up in 1961, only to be followed in early 1963 by Ba'thi-led coups d'etat in both Syria and Iraq. Unity of Arab states being a fundamental policy of this party, the two countries quickly entered into negotiations with Egypt for a tripartite union (which ultimately failed). Jordanians, especially Palestinian Jordanians, were once more caught up in the unity fervor. Inter alia, the parliament forced a debate on the subject: Prime Minister Samir Rifai, a Hashemite loyalist, spoke equivocally on the subject, while a large majority of the elected body, including nine of thirty members from the East Bank, emphatically favored some form of union. The government fell, but the king asked another long-term loyalist, his uncle Sharif Husayn Ibn Nasir, to form a government, which oversaw new elections in July 1963. Like the elections of 1961, these were strongly controlled (See Chapter 6).

While Arab anti-Israeli rhetoric had certainly been harsh during the 1950s and early 1960s, Arab actions had not for the most part been fundamentally threatening to the new state. Actions in 1964 by both Israel and Arab states, however, caused this pattern to change, and the first steps leading to the Arab-Israeli 1967 war were taken. Jordan was caught up in all phases of this dynamic because of its long border with Israel, because a large portion of its population was Palestinian, and because of pressures from its more "progressive" or "radical" neighbors, despite the king's more conservative worldview, to join in the common effort.

In early 1964, Arab governments became seriously concerned about Israel's intention to divert waters from the Sea of Galilee (also known as Lake Tiberas) for irrigation in the Negev Desrt. A scheme for an equitable division of the waters of the Jordan River (which feeds the Sea of Galilee and, further down, the Dead Sea) among the riparian states dates back to the 1954 Johnston Plan, which had been drawn up under the auspices of the Eisenhower administration. Israel had agreed to the plan, as had Jordan, technically, but it was never officially ratified by any Arab state. The 1964 problem arose because the Arab states, on the basis of technical data, believed that Israel intended to violate the draft Johnston Plan by taking a disproportionate share of sweet water from the north end of the Sea of Galilee rather than a balanced mixture of sweet and saline water from both ends of the sea.

To address the question, an Arab summit was held at which three actions were ratified. First, it was decided that the headwaters of the Jordan River in Lebanon and Syria were to be diverted.[14] Second, a unified Arab military command was created. And third, the Palestine Liberation Organization (PLO) was created. The first two actions had little effect on Jordan, but the last rapidly became a central issue and as of this writing still affects the country.

Within a short period, the PLO posed a challenge to Jordan internally and externally. Ahmad Shukairy, a fiery and often violent speaker, set up the organization in Jerusalem in 1964 and promptly undertook actions more appropriate to a state, that is, distributing arms and collecting taxes. In December 1964, Fatah, a Palestinian guerrilla organization, was established under the leadership of Yassir Arafat. Both organizations initiated various kinds of raids into Israel, mostly from Lebanon and Jordan, not from the more militant Syria. Such actions, in turn, created a serious military threat from Israel. Throughout the 1950s and early 1960s, it had been the policy of the Jordanian government and army to attempt to avoid border incidents by preventing villagers from infiltrating across the Israeli border. Even though this was an unpopular policy with the border villagers and among Palestinians generally, it was undertaken to prevent predictably harsh Israeli counterattacks and what would always be perceived as inadequate Jordanian military reponse (due to its decided inferiority to the Israeli military). The inadequate military response, in turn, would usually bring on political disturbances that the army would then be called on to quell, thus creating an oft-repeated, almost impossible scenario for the Jordanian regime. In sum, King Hussein's policy was by necessity diametrically opposed to the intentions of the PLO and Fatah.

From mid-1965, the border incidents became persistent enough that frequent and heavy Israeli counterattacks and preemptive attacks were experienced. In order to curtail these, the Jordanian government finally banned the PLO in the summer of 1966. This move increased the then heavy tension between Syria and Jordan and sparked sporadic border clashes between the two countries. Also, the airwaves were generally full of accusations and counteraccusations between the conservative states—Jordan and Saudi Arabia—and the progressive states—Iraq, Syria, and Egypt.

It should be noted that by the mid-1960s, Hashemite Jordan had drawn close to its former dynastic enemy, Saudi Arabia. They joined in a desire to preserve conservative, relatively pro-Western monarchies in the face of the threats from "radical" Arab nationalism and "communism." The relationship developed to the extent that the two countries exchanged territory on Jordan's southern border so that Jordan would have a longer coast line to develop south of Aqaba. Equally, Jordan often looked to Riyadh for advice and approval. In the late 1960s and 1970s, this relationship would evolve in a close, symbiotic manner.

Despite this Saudi support, the situation along the Israeli-Jordanian border remained precarious. Largely in response to Palestinian guerrilla raids across the Lebanese and Syrian borders, Israel on November 13, 1966, undertook a massive attack on the large West Bank village of al-Sumuʿ, destroying many of its houses and killing scores. Demonstrations against the Jordanian regime were instantaneous, and a higher level of tension was created inside Jordan and in the Middle East which, seemingly inevitably, slid into major war.

THE SECOND PHASE OF KING HUSSEIN'S REIGN: 1967-1974

If one were to rank the periods of King Hussein's reign, the seven years from 1967 to 1974 has to fall at the very bottom. It was initiated by overwhelming defeat and loss of territory and people at the hands of the Israeli military; it was marked in the middle by the dramatic events of civil war and a Syrian tank invasion; and it closed with an Arab summit meeting assigning the role of sole spokesman for the Palestinians to the Palestine Liberation Organization. The latter undermined King Hussein's role with his Palestinian-Jordanian citizens in the East Bank and the West Bank and his very claim to the Jordanian territory occupied by the Israeli military, namely the West Bank, including East Jerusalem. In addition, Jordan's economy was a shambles. Subsidies from other countries fluctuated considerably, largely as a function of Jordan's political fortunes; tourism and revenue from the fertile agriculture of the West Bank were lost; and political instability undermined investment. Despite these great difficulties, but with crucial help from friends in the Arab world and the West, the country and the regime were able to weather these problems.

During 1967, the level of violence continued to escalate. On April 7, Israel clashed with Syria on the ground and in the air; Syria sustained heavy losses. As part of the ongoing, rather bitter propaganda war, both Syria and Jordan ridiculed President Nasser for not ordering Egyptian forces to join in the battle and defend Arab land. After this goading, Egypt, in an increasingly reckless manner, started exchanging charges and countercharges and finally actions and counteractions with Israel. These included military maneuvers by both nations and Egypt's demands for the withdrawal of the UN Emergency Force from Sinai and the closing of the Straits of Tiran at the entrance to the Gulf of Aqaba to Israeli shipping. King Hussein, in a sudden about-face in the light of eminent danger to Arab lands, flew to Cairo on May 30 and put his small army under Egyptian command. Despite intensive diplomatic actions on the part of the United States and Europe, the situation continued to deteriorate. And on June 5, six days before the expiration of Israel's promise not to attack (at least as understood by the United States),[15] Israel launched a devastating preemptive attack on Egypt.

What followed was a spectacular and consummate Israeli military victory whose consequences may still be felt. The Egyptian army was

King Hussein.

roundly defeated, and the Sinai, in northeastern Egypt, was occupied. The Syrian army suffered the same fate, and the Golan Heights, in southwestern Syria, were occupied. Despite Israeli attempts to prevent it, Jordan, too, entered the battle and shelled West Jerusalem. The Israeli military retaliated, attacked Jordan's small air force, and captured the West Bank after some hard fighting in Jerusalem. Although Jordan's material losses were high, the army only lost 123 dead, despite earlier reports of much higher figures.[16]

This overwhelming defeat at the hands of Israel shook all the Arab countries in very fundamental ways. Their much-vaunted rhetoric was seen as so many empty sounds. People from students to intellectuals to the man in the street began questioning their very society and predicted necessary fundamental political changes. Jordan suffered the most. Nasser's Egypt lost prestige and a large stretch of desert containing some minerals, but this was a minor matter in comparison to Jordan's loss of the West Bank, which included one-third of its people, its richest agricultural land, the focus of its tourism, and the religious symbol of Jerusalem (holy to Islam and Christianity as well as to Judaism). In addition, into East Jordan flowed three hundred thousand refugees. And the Palestinians, considering that reliance on Arab states to regain their homeland had proved to be a bankrupt policy, turned to their own resources and quickly built up their guerrilla organizations, which would come to challenge King Hussein's authority.

On the regional and international fronts, two developments took place that were to influence strongly future events. In August 1967, an Arab summit was held in Khartoum at which "no" reigned. It was flatly decided that there would be no recognition of Israel and no negotiation with that country. The summit was followed by the famous November 22, 1967, UN Security Council Resolution 242, in which the basic principle of the exchange of territory for peace was established: "Withdrawal of Israeli armed forces from territories occupied in the recent conflict" was balanced with "termination of all claims or states of belligerency and respect for and acknowledgment of the sovereignty, territorial integrity and political independence of every State in the area and their right to live in peace within secure and recognized boundaries free from threats or acts of force." Obviously, the Arab summit and UN resolutions conflicted, and it took considerable time for the Arab countries to move toward an acceptance of UN Resolution 242.

On the Jordanian domestic scene, the situation progressively degenerated. The parliament had been recently elected, removing for some time the need to address the question of how it would handle elections with a large portion of the country under foreign military occupation. Cabinets rotated, with familiar faces from both the West and East banks holding ministries. The economy was a shambles. The West Bank and its resources were lost, development plans were severely disrupted, significant U.S. aid was halted because King Hussein had joined with President Nasser in saying the United States had aided Israel in the war[17], and general instability simply undermined economic confidence. One region of the country, the very productive Jordan Valley, was virtually depopulated in the 1968–1971 period due to Israeli shelling of guerrilla positions there. Finally, the country had again to absorb large numbers of Palestinian refugees albeit with the vital help of the UNRWA.

But it was the growth of the Palestinian guerrilla movement that would truly challenge the regime.[18] The guerrilla organizations and their attacks on Israel, although often thwarted, caught the imagination and often support of many throughout the Middle East, including Jordan. They enjoyed popularity even among the East Jordanian population for a while, and the king, who had recently lost a war, languished in public esteem. The Jordanian army suffered by comparison with the guerrillas, who were actually carrying out operations against the enemy while most often the army just observed. The movement grew and virtually developed into a state within a state, with considerable following in the Palestinian refugee camps and among some of the poorer quarters of Amman. At first, King Hussein did not attempt to control or stop it in a systematic way. Why? Most probably because he saw the real support the guerrillas enjoyed among a large segment of Jordan's people and, perhaps, out of some conviction that what they were doing was right. In one 1968 speech, he stated that one day all Jordanians might be guerrillas. But as the guerrillas' power grew, they became more arrogant and ostentatiously challenged the state and the army. As fundamental institutions came under attack, the king slowly changed his position.

The summer of 1970 was the climactic turning point. In June, a major clash between the army and the guerrillas occurred, but subsequently a new agreement was struck somewhat favorable to the Palestinian guerrilla organizations. The summer dragged on with sporadic acts of violence. At the time, U.S. Secretary of State William Rogers was trying to arrange a cease-fire along the Suez Canal between Egypt and Israel, which was realized in August. The guerrillas interpreted this move as particularly challenging to their policy of fighting for independence and as bolstering the states supposedly seeking some form of peace with Israel–Jordan and Egypt. The latter closed down the PLO's radio station in Cairo because it was continuously critical of Egypt's agreeing to the cease-fire.

Fatah was the strongest guerrilla group in the PLO and in Jordan, but it was George Habash's Popular Front for the Liberation of Palestine

(PFLP) that precipitated the civil war. Unlike Fatah, it called for the overthrow of the king and radical revolution. On September 6, the PFLP hijacked three airplanes. A TWA and a Swissair plane were flown to Dawson Field, an abandoned strip in Jordan's northeastern desert, and a Pam Am plane was flown to Cairo and destroyed. On September 9, another plane, BOAC this time, was added to the two in Dawson Field.

While negotiations to free the hostages were taking place at many levels in various countries, clashes between the army and guerrilla groups became more severe. King Hussein, however, was reluctant to undertake a full-fledged battle against the guerrillas whom, all things being equal, he knew his army could defeat. On one level, he most probably did not want to further divide his already disunited country. More immediately, he was unsure of the position of Iraq and Syria: Would they come to the aid of the guerrillas? This potential threat was quite real; following the 1967 war, between fifteen and twenty thousand Iraqi troops were stationed east of Amman (Saudi troops were in the south), and Syrian units were just north of the border. On another level, though, the king was witnessing the dismantlement of his country. And his army was extremely anxious to take action. If it did so without his orders, his authority and legitimacy would be undermined in the eyes of his officers and troops, the key to Hashemite survival.

The escalation of events finally caused King Hussein to take strong military action. On September 16, he appointed an all-military cabinet with Brigadier Mohammed Daoud as prime minister. General Habis al-Majaly, a protégé of the king's grandfather and a strongly loyal officer from Karak, was made commander of the army. The battle was fully joined.

The deteriorating events were being closely followed in the United States by President Nixon and his assistant for national security affairs, Henry Kissinger. As the crisis grew, Nixon denounced the guerrillas but, more important, sent elements of the Sixth Fleet to the eastern Mediterranean. (It should be noted that President Nasser pointedly did not support the guerrillas against the king.) As the crisis unfolded, the U.S. administration took additional military preparatory moves and initiated other actions designed to bolster the position of the imperiled king.[19]

Despite some preliminary worrisome noises, the Iraqi units based in Jordan did not support the guerrillas and even withdrew slightly, signaling their intention not to take any action. The Jordanian army was progressively successful against the Palestinian units in and around Amman. Most of the hijacked hostages were released, although all the aircraft had been destroyed earlier in the glare of world publicity. But on September 19–20, the Syrians invaded northern Jordan with a force of 200 tanks. Fearing a deteriorating battle front, King Hussein on

September 20 requested U.S. air strikes on the Syrian tanks. Over the next two tumultuous days, the king was to send mixed signals about what he wanted and from whom he wanted it. Initially, it appeared that Nixon wanted to use only U.S. forces in support of Jordan, but he eventually came around to the Kissinger position that the Israelis were better suited and positioned to help. As the Israelis were mobilizing on the Golan Heights, they contended that air and ground attacks would be necessary. The Jordanian king, however, was quite averse to having Israeli ground forces aid him (it would certainly have crossed his mind that it might be very difficult to rid his soil of these forces once they entered) and ambivalent about Israeli air support, preferring that of the United States.

All these questions became moot between September 22 and 24. On the twenty-second the Jordanian air force effectively took to battle, turning the tide decisively in Jordan's favor. On the twenty-fourth the Syrian tank force, or what was left of it, withdrew. The key to this success appears to have been the commitment of the air force. Why did the king finally take the gamble? Most probably, King Hussein decided to make the move partially because he finally had the assurance that the United States and Israel were behind him. Equally or perhaps more important, the Syrian air force was not committed to the battle for reasons that seem to be related more to Syrian internal politics than to a desire to help the Palestinians. An additional factor was the king's personal contacts with some Syrian factions, including, it is thought, the then Syrian air force commander, Hafez al-Assad, who subsequently seized power in a November 1970 coup d'etat.[20]

On September 26, King Hussein replaced his all-military cabinet with a mixed civilian-military one headed by long-time loyalist, but a hard-liner vis-à-vis the Palestinians, Wasfi al-Tal. And on September 27, King Hussein and Yassir Arafat, head of both the PLO and Fatah, signed a peace accord in Cairo that called for withdrawal of the guerrillas from the cities but allowed them to retain a presence in Jordan to continue the battle against Israel. President Nasser is credited with being very helpful in these negotiations. On the very day the agreements were concluded, this charismatic Arab leader died of a heart attack, leaving a great void in Arab leadership and once again allowing for a change of course in Arab history.

Over the following ten months, the army under the direction of Prime Minister Wasfi al-Tal undertook extensive and harsh mopping-up measures more in breach of the Cairo agreement than in conformance to it. The guerrilla units in Jordan were not only broken but for all practical purposes eliminated, the remnants moving on to Lebanon to fight from there. The Jordanian defeat of the Palestinians was not without its cost.

Kuwait and Libya cut off the aid accorded Jordan under the Khartoum summit; Syria closed its border and airspace to Jordan for a long period; the nation was generally shunned by the Arab world. And in September 1971, Prime Minister Wasfi al-Tal was assassinated by the Black September organization (named in memory of the September guerrilla defeat), which later proved to be an arm of Fatah. Not until the late 1970s could Yassir Arafat and King Hussein meet once more on even halfway friendly terms. Internally, the results were mixed. Most salient, the king's army stayed loyal. The Palestinians in it, numbering perhaps close to half of the total, did not desert. Admittedly, most of the strike units were still in East Jordanian hands. On the civilian side, bitterness remained but dissipated over the years. The West Bank, though, without direct Jordanian presence, moved progressively, but not entirely, away from the Jordanian regime. It developed its own internal dynamic, and many of its leaders stated that the PLO speaks for them.

Only slowly did Jordan raise itself out of the shambles of civil war. To address his Palestinian citizens' needs, King Hussein proposed a federation of the East Bank and the yet-to-be-liberated West Bank. Under this plan, there would be two regions, two capitals, and two parliaments, but only one foreign policy, one army, and one king. The PLO and anti-Hashemite leaders on the West Bank ridiculed the king's proposals, as did the Israeli prime minister, Golda Meir. At another level, once his financing allowed, the king resumed economic help for the West Bank. Jordan paid salaries to all government employees who were employed at the time of military occupation, modest funds were made available to municipalities, and the kingdom cooperated with Israel's "open bridges" policy, which allowed West Bank Palestinians and goods to move back and forth across the Jordan River. And the West Bankers continued to enjoy other privileges of Jordanian citizenship, such as passports and the right to buy property, set up businesses, and work for the government. Thus, despite civil war and military occupation, the Palestinian Jordanians still turned to the Hashemite regime because it controlled the functions and patronage of the state.

In Egypt, Anwar Sadat succeeded Gamel Abdal Nasser as president. His relations with the Arab world took on form and content considerably different from those of his predecessor. Rather than go over the heads of government directly to the people in other Arab countries as Nasser had, President Sadat dealt largely with governments. Additionally, he removed Soviet influence from his country and developed close relations with conservative regimes such as King Faisal's Saudi Arabia. In this atmosphere, at a September 1973 Cairo summit, King Faisal finally succeeded in reconciling the differences among the three front-line states, namely Egypt, Jordan, and Syria. This was to prove exceptionally important when Egypt and Syria launched a well-coordinated attack on Israel on October 6, 1973, in an attempt to regain land captured from them in 1967. King Hussein did not join the battle at first, but Jordan eventually contributed a few thousand men in an armored unit to the Syrian front on the Golan Heights. No Jordanian front was opened, and the Jordanian air force was not called into action.

After the war Secretary of State Kissinger engaged in his famous shuttle diplomacy and was successful in midwifing disengagement agreements on both the Egyptian and Syrian fronts. Thus, he helped the United States's new-found friend, Egypt, and its long-time critic, Syria. However, its old friend, Jordan, did not benefit. Secretary Kissinger's efforts with respect to the West Bank were not nearly as extensive as those on the Syrian front, and they failed utterly.

This bleak period, stretching from 1967 through 1974, was capped by quite successful PLO maneuvering on the regional and international levels. The Rabat summit of Arab heads of state, which was held in October 1974, declared that the PLO was the sole legitimate representative of the Palestinian people. Although this resolution cut King Hussein out of a role the Hashemites occasionally asserted, when faced with the unanimous position of all Arab countries, he could only accept the resolution. Jordan's right to negotiate the return of the West Bank was thus strongly undermined. And PLO chairman Yassir Arafat's invitation to address the UN General Assembly in November 1974 further underlined this message.

NOTES

1. Uda al-Qasus, "Memoirs" (in Arabic), unpublished memoirs of a leader of such horsemen, written in the 1920s.

2. Included among these officers was Lawrence of Arabia (T. E. Lawrence), who described his role in the revolt, although numerous aspects of his description are subject to doubt, in Seven Pillars of Wisdom (Garden City, N.Y.: Doubleday, 1935).

3. For material that more fully describes this revolt and the brief Arab kingdoms and their relationship to Britain, France, and the Zionist movement, see Sir Alec Kirkbride, A Crackle of Thorns (London: John Murray, 1976); Munib al-Mady and Sulayman Musa, Taʾrikh alʾUrdun fi al-Qarn al-ʿIshrin [History of Jordan in the twentieth century] (Amman?, 1959); Frederick G. Peake, History and Tribes of Jordan (Coral Gables, Fla.: University of Miami Press, 1958); Benjamin Shwadran, Jordan: A State of Tension (New York: Council for Middle Eastern Affairs Press, 1976).

4. C. S. Jarvis, Arab Command: The Biography of F. G. Peake Pasha (London: Hutchinson & Co., 1943), p. 61.

5. al-Mady, Munib, and Musa, Sulayman, *Taʾrikh alʾUrdun . . .*, pp. 279-280.

6. Kamel S. Abu Jaber, "The Legislature of the Hashemite Kingdom of Jordan," *Muslim World*, July-October 1969, pp. 220-250.

7. Quoted in Benjamin Shwadran, *Jordan*, p. 246.

8. John Bagot Glubb, *A Soldier with the Arabs* (New York: Harper & Brothers, 1957), pp. 155-166.

9. Cited in Shwadran, *Jordan*, p. 297.

10. The al-Rifai family is of Palestinian origin, but came to Transjordan in the interwar period and has been strongly loyal to the Hashemites since then.

11. A few purely Jordanian parties also existed.

12. See Peter Gubser, *Politics and Change in Al-Karak, Jordan* (London: Oxford University Press, 1973), pp. 135-139.

13. For an excellent description of these events, see P. J. Vatikiotis, *Politics and the Military in Jordan: A Study of the Arab Legion, 1921-1957* (New York: Praeger Publishers, 1967), pp. 127-131.

14. If realized, such a water diversion would have been a clear casus belli for Israel.

15. This promise was based on there being no changes in the situation on the ground. The bringing of Jordan's army under Egyptian command could definitely be interpreted as changing the status quo.

16. Personal communications from the late U.S. military attaché in Jordan, Major Robert Perry. Major Perry was killed in Amman in June 1970, during one of the flare-ups between the Jordanian army and the Palestinian guerrillas.

17. The accusation was later retracted on the basis that it been caused by faulty communications and radar readings.

18. For an excellent study of the guerrilla movement, see William B. Quandt et al., *The Politics of Palestinian Nationalism*, (Berkeley: University of California Press, 1973).

19. This Jordanian crisis, in the view of Nixon and Kissinger, was a very important test of the United States's ability to control world events. And in Kissinger's version of the September crisis, the United States was the maker and shaker of its solution. With only slight lip service to the efforts of Jordan, his narration makes it appear that it was the United States that brought events to a favorable conclusion. Although the United States certainly played an important role in support of the king and his regime, it would appear from the evidence that the crucial roles were played by the Jordanian army, the king, and his aides. See Henry Kissinger, *White House Years* (Boston: Little, Brown and Co., 1979), pp. 569-631.

20. See L. Dean Brown's perceptive review (*Middle East Journal*, Autumn 1978, p. 478) of William B. Quandt, *Decade of Decisions: American Policy Toward the Arab-Israeli Conflict, 1967-1976* (Berkeley: University of California Press, 1977), of which see pp. 105-127.

6

Contemporary Politics and International Relations

The middle and late 1970s constituted a period of relative calm for Jordan in both domestic politics and foreign relations. But in social and economic terms considerable change occurred. Thus, everything from communications, factories, and universities to health standards, agricultural productivity, and tourism experienced considerable progress. Per capita annual income, an imprecise but often used indicator, rose to a remarkable $1,000. Jordanians are found throughout Arab countries in government service, in business, and as technical experts. And in fall 1980 Jordan, once vilified for the September 1970–1971 civil war and shunned by many Arab countries, hosted a summit conference for the heads of most Arab states as King Hussein took on more influence in the region. In sum, recent history has been relatively kind to the country.

INTERNAL DEVELOPMENTS

The fallout from the Rabat summit decision temporarily set back King Hussein in his relations with his Palestinian-Jordanian citizens. At the time, it was reported that Crown Prince Hassan, the king's brother, along with some conservative East Bank Jordanians, argued that Jordan should forgo any claim to or help for the West Bank and its population, that the ties should be cut, and that the Hashemites should settle for the East Bank. The king did not accept this drastic position, but steps were temporarily taken that tended to call into question the future role of the Palestinian-Jordanians in Jordanian national life. On November 23, 1974, parliament, which was composed of an equal number of West and East Bankers, was dissolved by the king and a new cabinet was formed by Zaid Rifai. Only three of the nineteen cabinet members were Palestinian, rather than the usual six or seven. And Palestinians were warned to be good citizens or their status might change to simply being guests in the country.

As King Hussein's internal and regional fortunes improved, the government's view of the country's Palestinians altered. The number of Palestinians in the cabinet returned to normal. In February 1976, parliament was recalled, and many of the members who originated from the West Bank attended. This action was taken so that parliament could legally and indefinitely suspend elections, which had been scheduled for the following month. This was done because the question of excluding or including the West Bank in such elections could not be resolved. To exclude the West Bank would have meant giving in completely to the Rabat decision and implying forfeiture of Jordan's sovereign claim to the territory. It should be remembered that in adhering to the Rabat resolution, the king had said only that the PLO represents the Palestinians; he did not disclaim sovereignty over the West Bank. Yet Israel still militarily occupied the territory, and it was most probably impossible to hold Jordanian parliamentary elections there.

As a sign of tangible and continuing interest in the West Bank, the Office of Occupied Territories, reporting directly to the prime minister, was opened. Not only did the office help West Bankers with personal status affairs and look after Jordanian government employees who stayed on after June 1967, but it also administered a modest economic development program with West Bank municipalities, cooperatives, schools, and charitable societies. (This program was to increase in size considerably after the Israeli-Egyptian peace treaty was signed.) And the "open bridges" policy continued: West Bank Palestinians were free to travel back and forth across the Jordan River. In this manner, they were able to sustain considerable social, economic, and governmental relations with the East Bank, where most have relatives if not businesses.

That King Hussein was not persuaded to sever connections with the West Bank and its population is not surprising. Like his grandfather, King Abdullah, he has a sense of Arab nationalism that does not allow him to focus solely on parochial, Amman-centered interests. And as a Hashemite descendant of the Prophet Muhammad, he feels a duty to defend the holy city of Jerusalem. Additionally, a vivid youthful memory of his grandfather's assassination at the grand mosque of Jerusalem undoubtedly reinforces the king's attachment to the West Bank and especially Jerusalem. Finally, it is only natural that King Hussein does not want to go down in history as the Arab Muslim leader who lost Jerusalem in war and then proceeded to drop all claims and ties to it.

The Palestinians in the East Bank have not tried to challenge the regime in any major way since the 1970–1971 violence. As has been noted, many Palestinians occupy relatively high positions in government, but they cannot hope to attain the highest or more sensitive civilian or military positions. Much more important for bringing the

Palestinians into a relatively positive relationship to the state has been the comparatively unrestrictive economic atmosphere and the successive years of sustained economic growth in the post-1974 period. In this atmosphere, the Palestinian-Jordanian population has prospered. Additionally, Jordan's security offices keep a close watch on any incipient serious dissent and attempt to eliminate or contain it at its early stages. Thus, on balance, in the early 1980s there seemed little chance for popular resistance similar to that of a decade earlier.

Aside from the Palestinian issue per se, and partially because of it, there has been little political development at the national level in Jordan, in contrast to the much more rapid economic and social development. For one, Jordan now lacks an elected parliament. After the 1967 parliament was dismissed in 1974 and redismissed in 1976, no national body existed for two years, until the National Consultative Council of sixty members was appointed by the king in the summer of 1978. (This body is drawn from the East Bank population but includes many Palestinians who originate from the West Bank.) Although the council has no official legislative functions, there is a gentleman's agreement that the king and cabinet will not promulgate any new law not approved by the council.

With the lack of a true parliament, it is not surprising that the cabinet has been relatively stable, with only occasional reshuffles. From 1973 through 1976, Zaid Rifai, son of the late Samir Rifai, who was often prime minister in the 1940s and 1950s, occupied the prime ministership; Mudar Badran held the post from 1976 through 1979 and from 1980 to the time of this writing. Sharif Abdul Hamid Sharaf, a member of a collateral branch of the Hashemite family and close adviser to King Hussein, was briefly prime minister from December 1979 until his untimely death in July 1980. He was followed by Qasim Rimawi, the deputy prime minister and a Palestinian, to be replaced by Badran two months later. The composition of the cabinet basically reflected the sustained predominance of East Jordanians, but also a continued representation of people of West Bank origin. In addition, both regions and salient professional economic interests are consistently represented in the cabinet.

Political parties continued to be outlawed in the early 1980s, with the exception of the Muslim Brotherhood. The king allowed this fundamentalist religious party to remain active because of its past support for him and its role as a safety valve for fervent Muslims. The Muslim Brotherhood was consistently on the side of the king in the crises of the 1950s, 1967, and 1970–1971 and during his isolation in the early 1970s. Jordanian Muslims who felt a need to express their religious beliefs outside the mosque were able to do so through the Muslim Brotherhood. When the Ayatollah Khomeini came to power in Iran and shook the social structure of other countries, Jordan retained its stability. Basically, through the Muslim Brotherhood and other forms of expression, these feelings and energies had already been defused in the country. It should be added that the organization's membership is not exceptionally large and that many Jordanians are suspicious of it precisely because it is the only "party" allowed by the regime.

The military retains its strong loyalty to the throne. With more than a hundred thousand men, it represents a significant proportion of the labor force and population. Thus, the king pays very special attention to the military and its needs. He visits the bases frequently, and these visits are publicized in the media. And not only does he keep in close communication with the officer corps, but he also has contact with the ordinary soldier. In some years he will make an effort to shake the hand of every individual soldier – and not just lined up at attention, but in small groups so that he can have informal conversations with them. The military continues to be a means of upward mobility for bedouin from the desert, villagers from the countryside, and the poor of the cities. In other developing countries, there is often little for ex-soldiers and especially ex-officers to do. In Jordan, this problem has been largely avoided. The prosperous economy of the country and the booming economies of neighboring oil-producing countries have snapped up the retired soldiers, who usually possess useful skills. Officers have been encouraged to avoid retired officers' clubs, which are considered centers of unproductive activity at best and of political discontent at worst, and to enter into business, especially the construction business, a booming sector of the economy.

Despite the generally stable position of the military, it did react negatively when salaries did not keep up with inflation. Thus in 1973, 1974, and 1977, there were problems in the camps – not nation-threatening actions, but rather openly and strongly expressed disgruntlement. On each occasion, the government quickly met the expressed demands, which reflected not only the soldiers' thinking but also that of their families. In fact, to address the 1973 and 1974 problems, the government controlled the price of wheat so harshly that it created disincentives for farmers to produce the commodity, other than for home consumption. This distortion was largely alleviated by the late 1970s.

Other groups also participate in the noninstitutionalized decision-making process, which may be characterized as politics by consensus. For example, higher-level military officers form a noncorporate group that would advocate certain kinds of policies relating to the army and national security. Other groups playing roles would be small merchants of the bazaar, large merchants, small and large manufacturers, members of the bureaucracy, university professors and other professionals, rural leaders, and so forth. The issues debated are the normal ones, such as import tariffs, salary levels, direction or emphasis of development planning and projects, and in times of crisis, national honor and direction. Some of the groups have actual "nonpolitical" formal organizations, such as the syndicates or various clubs; others have no formal organizations but a kind of a natural leadership. Each group's leaders, in the appropriate forum, advocate positions beneficial to their respective groups. The appropriate fora would be the upper levels of ministries and planning groups as well as the offices of Prince Hassan, and most important, King Hussein. Due to the lack of national elected bodies, one could compare King Hussein's *diwan* (court) in the 1970s and early 1980s to that of his grandfather, King Abdullah. In a way, it is a highly evolved traditional court with the practice of considerable access kept intact. Due to the growth in size of the country, however, a higher proportion of this access has to be indirect than was the case under Jordan's first king.

The Hashemites have always had an uneasy relationship to formal democratic institutions. Thus, in Amir Abdullah's time an early law of elections was abandoned, and the first parliament, indirectly elected, was soon dissolved by the amir. The 1950s and 1960s were not dissimilar. Parliamentary elections were either rigidly regulated or, if a measure of freedom of choice was allowed, the parliament was soon brought under control—for example, by changing members—or it was simply dismissed. By the 1970s, King Hussein, admittedly in unique circumstances, turned to the thoroughly undemocratic means of appointing a quasi-parliament.

This lack of development of political institutions and formal political processes is ameliorated by the nonformal means of political access to the decision makers. Also, as noted below, the regime is now focusing on the development of local and regional institutions, some of which contain elected officials. Because the king pays considerable attention to all these matters and because Jordan's citizens have other ways in which they may expend their energies, e.g., in the economic arena, overt strain was not very notable in the late 1970s and early 1980s. But as events of the recent past have shown, the atmosphere can change quickly, and without formal structures and processes at the national level to match those developing at the local level and the economic and social growth, strains may become more overt.

In regional and local developments, new trends began to emerge in the middle and late 1970s. Municipal elections were held in the fall of 1976, the first since 1966. Men with technical education and some with a history of membership in the banned political parties took control of most municipalities, for the most part from older, more traditionally oriented leaders. This changing of the guard occurred with at least the tacit approval of the regime in Amman.

To complement this locally stimulated trend, the cabinet of Mudar Badran started holding cabinet meetings in all the provincial capitals. The purpose of the roving cabinet exercise was to demonstrate the government's interest in regional development and to attempt to counterbalance the bias toward Amman in the country's economic and social progress.

This campaign was followed by the creation of the more substantive regional development groups. The Jordan Valley Development Authority, the epitome of such groups had long existed. In 1978, legally constituted groups were created for both the Amman and Irbid areas, and others were slated for the remaining districts. These groups, which have or will have officers and staffs, are to address, in a regional context within the national plan, questions and programs relating to manpower, water resources, agriculture, industry, mining, tourism, transport, energy, telecommunications, and public utilities.[1] The formation and activities of these groups was accompanied by considerable publicity in the press and on radio and television.

When Abdul Hamid Sharaf became prime minister, decentralization took on a more articulated place in Jordanian policy. Describing this new emphasis, the prime minister said, "[It] is what you might call regionalisation in our local government, to give power back to the regional centres and the provinces, to give more power to the mayors and governors, and to allow the local communities everywhere to develop and to run their own affairs. And this covers the economic as well as the political side, because it is very necessary to allow the people to carry the burden and to share in the burden of government."[2] The mechanism for this new participation would be local institutions and large regional councils composed of mayors, village council heads, and civic leaders. These councils would have authority over regional aspects of the socioeconomic order and presumably the groups initiated under Prime Minister Badran's government.

Another aspect of this policy was to encourage more participation in development from the bottom—in planning *and* the provision of resources—than had been practiced in the past. This new trend, said the prime minister, "is not only necessary for us in terms of economic need, but it is also desired by our people. I think it is very unhealthy for the government to take a patronizing attitude to the people and to treat them as if they were only objects of service, not participants in the development process. We want to make this change both psychologically and in reality."[3]

This new policy, which is continued under Prime Minister Badran's government, represents a considerable departure from past practice. Thus, the National Planning Council, acting under the direction of the

prime minister, Prince Hassan, and King Hussein, has definitely conducted its business from the top down. The Jordan Valley Development
Authority, the only regional group until 1978, equally undertook planning and implementation from the top down. People were considered
primarily as "objects," to use Sharaf's word, of manpower plans and services. The devolution of authority to the people has long been officially
envisaged, but none of significance has occurred. Consequently, if
lessons from the past are salient, any meaningful participation at
regional levels will be long in coming.

A last political factor of importance is the nature of King Hussein's
legitimacy in the eyes of his people.[4] Those factors that give him
legitimacy vary to some degree from group to group. First, having led the
great revolt against the Ottoman Empire, the Hashemites have substantial claim to being among the most important initiators and sustainers of
the Arab nationalist movement. King Hussein has a special feeling for
and a sense of duty toward the larger Arab cause he often invokes. King
Hussein's conception of Arab nationalism is not the total Arab political
unity in a single state often advocated by others, but a strong cultural,
social, and economic relationship among the various Arab states and
peoples that will make the whole more than the sum of its parts. Second,
the Hashemites claim legitimacy on the basis of religious feeling. Thus,
King Hussein is the scion of the family of the Prophet Muhammad, an inheritance that is especially important to his more conservative citizens.

Third, the king is perceived as being honestly interested in – and
capable of promoting – the economic and social development of all his
people. In this regard, notably from 1975, Jordanians have increasingly
enjoyed the benefits of this development. At the minimum, development
has coopted many people to the regime if it did not add to or create
legitimacy for the monarch. A related factor – and an important one
when Jordanians compare their nation to others in the Arab world – is
the atmosphere of relative personal and economic freedom. The state
under King Hussein's leadership has created an environment in which
people feel they may personally advance and feel personally secure. The
urban poor feel the impact of this the least, but even they have progressed in the last few years, although not as fast as those from other
strata. Fourth, the king enjoys a perception of strength of character in the
face of major challenges, and his very survival in face of many adversi-
ties from the 1950s through the early 1970s, and his longevity on the
throne, form another legitimizing element. Finally, most Jordanians find
him to be personally attractive. He speaks eloquent Arabic, he is thought
by most to be personally honest, he possesses those honored qualities of
courage and daring, and he obviously meets and relates to other heads of
states as an equal.

Attending services at a mosque: (left to right) Shaykh Abdullah Ghoshen, King Hussein, Prince Muhammad, and Crown Prince Hassan.

The king today has, in a decidedly unstable Middle East, a relatively stable throne due to his perceived legitimacy—and his ever-loyal army. But his claim to legitimacy was not always strong. It had to be developed and nurtured. In the 1950s, the country was in tumult and his legitimacy was often challenged. In the aftermath of 1967, he did not enjoy popularity because he had lost the war. This was true not only among Palestinians who had lost the West Bank, but also among some East Bankers for whom, as with others in the Middle East, prowess in arms is honored. As the 1970s progressed, however, earlier weakness and challenges were overcome as both the country and the monarch continued to mature.

JORDAN IN THE ARAB WORLD

A small, somewhat vulnerable country, Jordan is not a maker and shaker in regional or international affairs. Recognizing the country's limitations, King Hussein and his advisers have continuously attempted to seek out patrons while avoiding what might be dangerous commitments in the changing pattern of associations and alliances among countries in the Middle East. In earlier days his grandfather had relied on the British as patron. As King Hussein cut this tie in the mid-1950s, he turned to the United States for various forms of aid. (During the period after the 1967 war, when relations with the United States were not of the warmest, King Hussein briefly turned for military advice to Pakistan, with which he retains close ties.) Even though the financial aid flowing from the Arab countries now dwarfs that from the United States, Jordan retains the U.S. link, although at times it is strained, while he cultivates European ties, both on a bilateral basis and through the European Economic Community.

Until 1958, with occasional lapses, Jordan's closest Arab friend was Iraq, which was then ruled by a brother Hashemite ruling family. After the latter's overthrow, Jordan was essentially isolated until good relations with its once bitter dynastic foe, Saudi Arabia, developed in the 1960s. Although Saudi Arabia's support in terms of military defense might be weak, Jordan's southern neighbor is of considerable importance in terms of diplomacy and finances. Thus, after the 1970–1971 civil war, Saudi Arabia helped keep the country from being totally isolated in the Arab world and was the only Arab country to continue the important subsidies awarded at the Arab summit in Khartoum in 1967.

Until the early 1970s, Jordan was known – with reason – as one of the poor countries of the Middle East. It constantly needed financial resources, was full of unemployed refugees, and needed help to defend its long border with Israel; its very existence was often questioned. From the mid-1970s, this image and reality changed, with no small effect on the country's relations with its neighbors. Although still in need of financial resources for its ambitious development program, it finally had some revenue-producing resources of its own: operating phosphate mines (with high world prices for phosphate) and vegetable and citrus production in the Jordan Valley.

Of most importance, however, are Jordan's human resources. This country's efforts at education and the efforts of the UNRWA started paying off in substantial and tangible ways in the 1970s. And this effect was magnified by the partial crippling of Lebanon's rich manpower resources due to that country's civil war. Taking advantage of this opportunity, Jordanians now working in the oil-producing countries are sending back very substantial remittances to Jordan. In turn, they are providing services that are both valuable and visible. For example, they run and provide the technical backup for television systems; design university programs, from curricula to credit-hour systems; and program and operate computers. Of substantial importance to many of the small countries along the Arabian Gulf littoral and from time to time in Oman and North Yemen are seconded or retired Jordanian military personnel and police officials. They fill many vital posts and have played a key role in training efforts. In this manner, Jordan has been able to contribute substantially to the internal stability of these countries and to Arabian Gulf security. And its new regional technical role is translated not only into individual remittances, but also into bilateral transfers from oil-producing countries for Jordan's defense and development efforts as well as a certain influence in the affairs of these countries.

Within the borders of Jordan, the country has developed another regional role, again filling to some extent the void created by the Lebanese civil war. Increasingly Jordan has begun to host meetings of various professional groups, from journalists to lawyers to rural health experts, as well as ministerial groups (e.g., meetings of all Arab ministers of agriculture). To cap this, Jordan hosted its first Arab summit meeting in November 1980 – not only an honor to the country, but also no mean political accomplishment on the part of King Hussein. A variety of inter-Arab meetings had long been occurring throughout the region, but their number grew demonstrably as the flow of funds in the Arab world increased after 1973, a time when Jordan was finally in a position to benefit from them.

This facilitating and participating role in inter-Arab meetings and development led to the formation in the aftermath of the November 1980 Arab summit of the Arab Thought Club, more familiarly known as the Club of Aqaba, after the location of the founding meeting. This new institution is a product of a conference called by Crown Prince Hassan and attended by thirty-five leading Arab participants, including such luminaries as Saudi Arabia's oil minister, Sheikh Ahmad Zaki Yamani; Dr. Burhan Dajani, secretary general of the Federation of Arab Chambers of Commerce; and Bashir Ibn Yahmad, publisher of *Jeune Afrique* magazine. The concept is that the club will be a "think tank" like the Club of Rome; it will provide Arab scholars, professionals, and intellectuals with the opportunity to address problems facing the entire Arab nation, "such as problems in the fields of labor, migration, technology, agriculture and food security, or education."[5] It is noteworthy in and of itself that Arab leaders wish to start such a forward-looking institution; for Jordan, it is quite important that Jordan took the lead in its formation and the others accept its location there.

Jordan built its relations with the Arab world in the 1970s in a three-pronged manner. First, in the pre–Camp David era, Jordan attempted to retain positive relations with Egypt, the largest and most powerful of the Arab states. Because Jordan shares no border with Egypt and because President Sadat's policies were relatively pragmatic, this was relatively easily achieved. After Camp David, however, relations soured, although in keeping with its normal practice, Jordan did not generally attack Egypt as many other Arab countires did. Second, King Hussein assiduously cultivates the oil-producing countries of the Arabian Gulf and Saudi Arabia. He (and his brother) travel there frequently – and the top and middle-level leaders of these countries often visit Jordan. As already noted, Jordan supplies many of these countries with highly skilled manpower for their security services. For the most part, their interests overlap, that is, they jointly perceive a mutual need to preserve the stability of the conservative and moderate regimes of the region. Their immediate national interests might differ somewhat; for Jordan, its western border with Israel and the various aspects of the Palestinian question are the most salient, while the others see internal stability and threats from Iran, at times Iraq, and other radical states as their most immediate concern. All worry about larger Soviet aspirations, but they certainly do not consider them to be behind all or even many of the problems they face. It should also be recalled that in the 1970s when the shah of Iran was still on his throne, King Hussein sought out his patronage, received aid from Iran, and cooperated with the shah in such ventures as defending the sultan of Oman's regime against the Dhofar rebellion.

Third, throughout the 1960s and early 1970s, Iraq and Syria were basically hostile to Jordan's Hashemite monarchy. After the 1973 Arab-Israeli war, King Hussein attempted, with mixed success, to change this negative pattern. The most prominent early development was with Syria or, more specifically, with President Assad, the general who had been head of the Syrian air force that had opted not to do battle with King Hussein's air force in 1970. In 1975, the two countries signed accords to cooperate in and coordinate defense, foreign affairs, economic policy, information, education, and cultural programs. The first two items were not given great emphasis, but the rest were. With respect to economic policy a joint "agreement exempts exports in both directions from customs duties and other . . . tariffs. Import licenses are waived and clearance procedures are simplified. Raw materials used by comparable industries [are] exempt from duty, to give . . . equal competition in Syrian and Jordanian markets."[6] Joint free industrial zones and joint companies have been established. Also, single curricula for schools have been written, with reliance primarily on the Jordanian model. On December 8, 1976, in accordance with the spirit of Arab unity, the two countries announced their intention to form a union; little ever came of this agreement, however. Additionally, the heads of state have exchanged visits from time to time and they have coordinated their respective foreign policies somewhat.

At the same time, Jordan's overt relations with what was generally described as "radical" Iraq were poor. Criticism and hostile words were occasionally exchanged, and Jordanian university students in Iraqi universities were at times harassed. However, the countries were developing a lively economic relationship. Jordan exported agricultural produce to Iraq, but more important, Iraq was giving Jordan substantial aid to develop the port of Aqaba and the country's road system. Iraq was interested in access to Jordan's port as an alternative to its vulnerable and poor ports on the Gulf and to transporting imports across Syria, with which it was often at serious odds. Jordan wanted to receive development aid and to have alternative potential friends in case relations with Syria soured.

By 1980, Jordan's relationships with Syria and Iraq had virtually reversed themselves. Jordan was materially and politically supporting Iraq in its war against Iran, but relations with Syria had become hostile. During 1979, Syria had increasingly turned against Jordan, largely due to its own quite serious internal problems. For a series of domestic reasons, the Muslim Brotherhood had conducted a series of attacks against Syrian state institutions. President Assad subsequently attacked Jordan verbally, asserting that the country aided and abetted the Muslim Brotherhood and allowed it to set up guerrilla camps on Jordanian soil. He demanded that Jordan curtail the organization's activities. Well-informed sources state that Syria had no solid intelligence to prove Jordan's involvement but basically felt forced to attack Jordan to create an outside focus for its problems. It is obvious, though, that King Hussein would not crack down on the ordinary activities in Jordan of the Muslim Brotherhood – a legal organization in the country – because of its past effective support of his regime. A less important factor contributing to these tensions is the fundamentally different orientations of the two countries. Syria is vocally (perhaps not substantively) pro-PLO; conducts occasional air battles with Israel; avows radical, at times socialist, positions; and is close to the Soviets. Jordan is close to the conservative and moderate Arab regimes, competes with the PLO at certain times, maintains a peaceful border with Israel, and is basically pro-Western.

The strife between the two countries escalated when in September 1980 Jordan threw its strong support behind Iraq in the latter's war against Iran. This Jordanian action was especially provoking to Syria because of strong Iraqi-Syrian enmity. Syria actually joined Libya in supporting Iran against its Arab brother. It was in this atmosphere that the November Arab summit was to take place. Failing to sway a majority of the Arab states to call for its postponement, Syria led Libya, the PLO, Lebanon, Algeria, and South Yemen in a boycott of the summit. And to further heighten tensions, Syria drew up its forces on the Jordanian border, forcing King Hussein to do likewise. In the spring of 1981, troops were withdrawn from the border and the harsh exchanges started to subside, partly as a consequence of mediation by a Saudi Arabian leader, Prince Abdullah. However, economic relations had been maintained throughout the standoff; trade continued and contracts for joint industries were let–again not unlike Iraqi-Jordanian relations in the mid-1970s.

King Hussein's reasons for overtly backing Iraq in its war with Iran and for taking the lead in persuading others to lend their support are varied. One is definitely Iraqi aid, which was raised considerably, in conjunction with that from Saudi Arabia, at the 1978 Arab summit (see below) to a level of almost $1 billion a year. Second, Syria's increasingly vitriolic treatment of Jordan has driven the king to seek an alternative patron in the region, and Iraq, especially as it was moderating its formerly radical positions, had the necessary qualifications. Third, it would appear obvious (although it was not mentioned in published sources) that Iraq had some form of guaranteed access to the Aqaba port, especially in crucial times such as war when its only seaport would be threatened or actually closed. Fourth, King Hussein's sense of Arab duty played a role. Thus, during the early stages of the war, the king publicly justified his strong support of Iraq and his urging of support by others by saying: "Iraq is our depth. If Iraq is facing danger there, we are facing it here. We stand on the side of our brothers and support them with all our capabilities and resources."[7] This statement strongly implies that Jordan expects support from Iraq in its future conflicts. Finally, the king stands to benefit from the fruits of the war. In 1980–1981, Iraq has turned over around fifty U.S.-built M60 tanks it captured from Iran, allowing Jordan to postpone the purchase of these tanks from the United States.

That King Hussein so strongly and substantially supported Iraq despite warnings from Washington that such action could be counterproductive is indicative of Jordan's new position in the Arab world in the early 1980s. For one thing, Arab aid eclipses anything coming from the West. And although the king still decidedly values his strong U.S. and European connections, his Arab friends and their potential help have come to rival–in a friendly way–his Western connections. In addition, in the years following Secretary of State Kissinger's failure to address Jordanian-Israeli disengagement as seriously as he had Israeli disengagement with Egypt and Syria, Jordan and the United States have frequently experienced fundamental differences on policy.

REGIONAL AND INTERNATIONAL RELATIONS

Jordan's relations with Israel are inextricably combined with its relations with the Palestinians and stem from incompatible claims of Israel and the Palestinians to the same land. Jordan's policy toward Israel has been relatively consistent. Tactically, it attempts to maintain a peaceful border with the country, knowing full well that Israel's military is far superior to its own. This policy has been retained, except for a short period between 1967 and 1970, despite its considerable lack of popularity among certain segments of the Palestinian population and certain Arab countries. Strategically, Jordan has long accepted the fact of Israel's existence, readily accepted UN Resolution 242, and most important, advocates the resolution of the Arab-Israel conflict in a just and comprehensive manner.

Official policy toward the Palestinians has also been basically consistent. Thus, in 1950, when parliament unified the East and West banks, it explicitly stated that this unity was without prejudice to "the final settlement of Palestine's just case within the sphere of national aspirations." In spring 1981, Adnan Abu Odeh, Jordan's minister of information and often King Hussein's senior spokesman on such matters, reiterated the Jordanian policy toward peace and the Palestinians in a more broadly articulated fashion:

Principles of Jordanian Policy
Jordan continues to believe in the necessity of reaching a peaceful solution to the Middle East crisis. Such a solution must be based on the total withdrawal of Israel from the occupied Arab lands, especially Arab Jerusalem. In return, reasonable security guarantees acceptable to Israel and the other Arab states must be provided. Jordan considers such a peaceful solution possible only if the basic issues of the conflict are addressed. Discussion of the consequences of continued Israeli occupation of the disputed areas is a dangerous exercise.

Any peaceful solution must be comprehensive. All immediate parties to the conflict, including Jordan, Syria, Lebanon, and the PLO (as the sole legal representative of the Palestinian people), along with the United States, the Soviet Union, and the European Community, must participate in any such solution within the framework of the United Nations.

The PLO is the legitimate interlocutor for the Palestinians. On numerous occasions King Hussein has said that Jordan will not act as a substitute for the PLO, but rather as a source of support for it. The PLO has no national competitor that could replace it. Jordan believes that the PLO, which has proved that it mirrors the aspirations of the Palestinian people, is capable of representing their interests once discussion of the crisis is conducted on a just and balanced basis.

Jordan belives that merely avoiding war does not ensure peace. The present "phony peace" actually makes the area vulnerable to upheaval. A resolution of the crisis requires a permanent peace rather than a fragile, illusive and imbalanced peace that carries the potential for eventual new wars that could result in the Arab character of the region being replaced by a foreign one. Thus it is imperative to solve the current problems by adopting an approach different from that of the Camp David Accords, which have not only failed but have become an obstacle to peace.[8]

More specifically, on the issue of the Palestinians' future, King Hussein stated: "The key issue that must be addressed here is the right of self-determination. This right is endorsed and accepted by this country [United States] and by our fundamental international philosophy in this age, but is strangled by reservations when it comes to the Palestinian people."[9] Abu Odeh added: "As Jordan sees it, self-determination means possession by the Palestinians of the freedom and rights specified by the Human Rights Charter. These freedoms encompass the social, cultural, and economic rights necessary for free political self-expression."[10]

Jordan's policy may not have been so explicit before the 1974 Rabat summit, but since 1974 the king and other Jordanian leaders have repeatedly restated this position. It should be made clear, though, that advocating self-determination and calling the PLO the legitimate representative of the Palestinians is not the same as advocating the establishment of an independent Palestinian state in the West Bank (and Gaza). Rather this position is much more an advocacy of giving the Palestinians some form of choice as to their future. Ideally this choice would be among total independence of the West Bank (including East Jerusalem) and Gaza, some form of attachment to Jordan, or some form of attachment to Israel. Jordan's preference—and one would imagine a strong one—would be the second option. In a discussion of the Palestinians' attempt "to achieve their national identity on Palestinian soil," Abu Odeh easily put this effort in a Jordanian context: "Contrary to what many claim, Jordan took the lead in underscoring Palestinian identity when it proposed in 1972 a United Arab Kingdom to be created after Israeli withdrawal and the establishment of peace. The kingdom was to be comprised of a federation between a Palestinian region and a Jordanian region after a plebiscite in the two regions."[11] In sum, Jordan's policy is based on a search for a just and comprehensive peace that inherently includes the basic right of self-determination for the Palestinian people. In addition, on the basis of some form of choice and with the blessing of some Arab countries, Jordan would strongly prefer having the West Bank under its wing once again.

Since 1974, Jordan has been involved to varying degrees in attempts to secure the release of the West Bank from Israeli military occupation. It was reported that in 1975 and 1976 Jordan and Israel undertook secret talks in one form or another but that they were eventually broken off. Apparently, Israel's offer, which is most probably what was known as the Allon Plan, named for Israeli Foreign Minister Yigal Allon, did not meet Jordan's minimal requirements. This plan proposed, inter alia, that Israel would return to Jordan most of the population and about 70 percent of the land of the West Bank but would retain possession of and a military presence in the balance of the land, including a strip along the Jordan River. The latter provision meant that Jordanian citizens who wished to cross between the West and East banks would have to go through Israeli checkpoints. Obviously, this provision would have been unacceptable to the king, as would have been the alienation of a full 30 percent of West Bank land.

Relations with the United States have not always been smooth. President Carter's administration began inauspiciously. In February 1977, shortly before Secretary of State Cyrus Vance's initial trip to Jordan and other Middle Eastern countries, it was reported in the *Washington Post* that the Central Intelligence Agency had for years been making secret payments to King Hussein. The Jordanian government indignantly denied the report, and Jordanian leaders easily shrugged it off, but the bitterness remained. Naturally, rumors circulated about the true intent and motivation behind this "leak," which was generally seen as an attempt to poison relations between Jordan and the new administration.

Then, within the context of attempting to convene a Geneva peace conference that would bring all parties to the Arab-Israeli conflict together in search of a comprehensive solution, the Carter administration began making strong overtures to the PLO, an action that could only disquiet Jordan. President Carter called for a Palestinian homeland and sent the PLO a multitude of signals about how it could obtain a seat at the peace conference. At one stage, he virtually drafted acceptable phraseology for the PLO's acceptance and qualification of UN Resolution 242 so that it could obtain U.S. support for its attendance at the conference.[12] This and other steps toward Geneva were decisively interrupted in November 1977 when President Anwar Sadat made his dramatic, courageous, and historic trip to Jerusalem, where he addressed the Israeli Knesset (parliament). This move successfully undermined the comprehensive approach and the focus on the Palestinians and returned the diplomatic search to the old Kissinger-style step-by-step process. The culmination was the much-discussed September 1978 Camp David Agreements and the 1979 peace treaty between Egypt and Israel.

In this process Jordan was at one time forgotten or bypassed and then haughtily included in the agreement without its consent or substantive consultation. Thus, President Carter's early cultivation of the PLO could only be seen by Jordan as undercutting the one Arab country with the longest record of close association with the West and as supporting Jordan's major competitor for the loyalty of the Palestinians in the West Bank and, to a lesser extent, on the East Bank. The United States also seemed blatantly insensitive to Jordan's acceptance and position in the Arab world.

The drama radically changed as U.S. overtures to the PLO failed and President Sadat went to Jerusalem. In early 1978, both Egypt and the United States attempted to draw King Hussein into the process, but to no avail. Although King Hussein did not condemn the Sadat initiative as did some of his Arab brothers – and often in severe and harsh terms – he was not able to join it unless it met his minimal terms, which, depending on his audience, variously included a modest "declaration of principles providing for 'Israeli withdrawal' from the West Bank (not necessarily total withdrawal) and a declaration of Palestinian rights" and a stronger position including "total withdrawal to the 1967 borders, including Israeli evacuation of East Jerusalem and self-determination for the Palestinians after withdrawal."[13] At Camp David, with King Hussein not attending and not consulted, Jordan was mentioned fifteen times in the section having to do with West Bank autonomy. Not only could the king not accept this truncated version of autonomy, but also he highly resented the presumption that he would meekly follow in step. That he was not even telephoned from Camp David about Jordan's inclusion rankled deeply. Even worse was National Security Advisor Zbigniew Brzezinski's flying trip to Jordan on which he presented the king for his approval with already prepared communiqués lauding the agreements. In reaction, the king's government soberly issued an alternative communiqué critical of the agreements and presented the U.S. administration with a series of written questions as to the meaning of the agreements.

In presuming King Hussein's acceptance of the Camp David Agreements and almost automatic participation in them, the Carter administration obviously overlooked some of King Hussein's basic constituencies and thus the direction he would have to take. In his constituency list, following close behind the Hashemite family and his loyal East Jordanians, are his Palestinian citizens and some of his Arab neighbors, notably Saudi Arabia and Syria in this case. His Palestinian citizens would have interpreted acceptance of this weak autonomy, which included no guarantee for return of the West Bank (and Gaza) to total Arab control, as a sellout. (Time appears to be proving the critics correct. Israeli settlement activity in the militarily occupied territories continues at an escalated pace, and the Begin government appears adamant against any Israeli withdrawal from the West Bank and Gaza Strip.[14]) Syria too did not trust this route to retrieval of occupied land and also was deeply mistrustful of President Sadat by this time. Saudi Arabia joined the rejection, seeing no chance of true deoccupation or any opportunity to regain the Muslim holy places in Jerusalem. The sum of these constituency views or positions is that King Hussein could not afford to join this Camp David "process." If the process had enjoyed more success—if the autonomy negotiations had in a timely fashion turned out an agreement that could be interpreted as promising for the Palestinians of the West Bank and Gaza Strip—the king might have been able to accept a role. This was not the case, however, as the autonomy talks foundered (remaining incomplete as of spring 1982, two years after the completion date stipulated in the Egyptian-Israeli peace treaty) and the Israelis built numerous new settlements in the militarily occupied territories, took considerably more land, and increasingly deprived Palestinians of decision-making rights in and control over their own institutions.

A somewhat related set of developments in the Jordan–United States–Israel triangle resulted from the summer 1981 elections in Israel and the April 1982 Israeli handing over of the last piece of Sinai to Egypt under the new Egyptian-Israeli peace treaty. After the elections, Prime Minister Begin formed a new cabinet that included Ariel Sharon as minister of defense. Sharon has long (since 1975) advocated the demise of the Hashemite monarchy so that the Palestinians may establish their own state in East Jordan; there would then be no need to form a Palestinian state in the West Bank, which he and other Israelis claim as part of Eretz Israel (Hebrew for "the land of Israel"). During the summer and early fall of 1981, Sharon pushed this theme so frequently and hard that the Jordanians became jittery, especially when an oral statement by President Ronald Reagan was misinterpreted to King Hussein to mean that President Reagan supported Sharon's plan. In response to this considerable Jordanian unease, the United States issued a statement in which it pointedly noted that the United States "remains committed to Jordan's stability, territorial integrity and security."[15] And by spring 1982, the United States seemed to be prepared to offer Jordan a package of sophisticated arms. Although these were not a match for Israel's arsenal, there were considerable Israeli objections to the pending arms deal.[16] The second worrisome challenge to Jordan was Prime Minister Begin's resurrected theme, adopted after the final withdrawal from Sinai, that the West Bank is not only part of Eretz Israel, it is part of *western* Eretz Israel, "thus reviving the notion of the Revisionist Zionist movement, to which he belongs, that the historical land of Israel also included the east bank of the Jordan River, currently Jordanian territory. . . . [For example] the hymn of Mr. Begin's underground Irgun Zvai Leumi . . . had asserted historical Jewish rights to both sides of the Jordan River."[17] While the Sharon and Begin plans or statements may be somewhat at odds or contradictory, the troublesome aspect for the regime in Jordan and most Jordanians is that its powerful western neighbor seems to be hinting at plans for Jordan that do not correspond to the desires or plans of Jordan itself.

It would be an understatement to say that the fallout in the rest of the Arab world from the major U.S. peace initiative was considerable. In November 1978, a major Arab summit, which Jordan attended, was held in Baghdad at which the comprehensive approach to peace was supported:

Having examined the situation in the Arab world and abroad, the conference reaffirmed the adherence of the Arab nation to a just peace based upon total Israeli withdrawal from all Arab lands occupied in 1967, including Arab Jerusalem, and reaffirmed the maintenance of the inalienable national rights of the Palestinian Arab people, including their right to return, to self-determination and to the establishment of an independent state on their national soil.[18]

Most salient in this key part of the summit statement was the de facto recognition of Israel implied in the phrase "Israeli withdrawal from all Arab land occupied in 1967" as part of the total peace package. Additionally, turning to a more narrow focus, the Baghdad summit awarded Jordan $1.25 billion in annual aid if it would not join the Camp David process — which it was not intending to do in any case. Through 1981 Jordan had actually received a little less than $1 billion as a consequence of the summit; it has been reported that in 1982 Jordan would receive up to $1.4 billion. Additionally, a joint Jordanian-PLO committee was set up to aid the Palestinians and their institutions in the West Bank and Gaza Strip. The committee was pledged $200 million, of which more than $60 million had actually been collected by fall 1980. Despite difficulties, some of the funds have entered the West Bank and Gaza Strip, where the Palestinians have used them for development purposes and some institutional support (municipalities, schools, and the like). By the spring of 1982 this flow had been seriously curtailed by actions of the Israeli military government in the occupied territories. Because of this aid, as well as similarity of policy, Jordan and the PLO drew closer in their working relationship, even though numerous strains were still apparent.

The Arab-Israeli conflict has affected economic as well as political development in Jordan. The next major step in Jordan's development program for the Jordan Valley has been held up. A number of small and medium-sized dams have already been constructed and feed the key canals and the rich agriculture. These dammed waters lie entirely within Jordan and thus raise no riparian rights issues. The next dam, and a very major one at that, is slated to be constructed on the Yarmouk River, on which Syria and Jordan enjoy riparian rights. Israel and the West Bank also have such rights, because both touch on the Jordan River of which the Yarmouk is a tributary. The United States in 1979–1980 attempted to negotiate secretly among the three sovereign parties to resolve the riparian shares so that Jordan and its international financiers (the World Bank, the United States, and Arab countries) could move forward to initiate the project,[19] but the first stage of bidding was repeatedly delayed, as the United States was unable to deliver an agreement. Part of the problem related to the share allotted to the West Bank and to which entity would have control over it, Israel or the future West Bank autonomous authority being negotiated by Israel and Egypt.

In the larger context of the search for a just and comprehensive peace in the Middle East, Jordan has not rested solely with being a member of the rejectionist group. Rather, King Hussein actively seeks a positive alternative. This alternative, although not entirely worked out, would include the principles outlined at the beginning of this section. King Hussein seeks a comprehensive peace on all fronts with Israel that would include withdrawal and guarantees for all parties. The method for achieving it rejects the narrow Camp David process and again looks to a comprehensive approach whereby the United States, the European Community, and the USSR would be brought in, recognizing that all have a role, all are in a position to play the role of broker, and that any one might undermine a comprehensive peace if not included. As informal spokesman for the moderate Arab countries, a status conferred on the king at the Amman summit of November 1980, the king and his leading representatives have increased their public advocacy of this comprehensive approach.[20]

A final word needs to be said about Jordan's relations with Europe. First, when seeking to pressure the United States or acceding to Arab countries' maneuverings in the Arab world, King Hussein makes approaches to the Soviet Union, but there appears to be little likelihood that Jordan would entertain a serious relationship with that country, given the king's strong anticommunist, moderate position and still quite close relations with the West. (In spring 1982, however, it was reported in the press that Jordan had announced the signing of an agreement with the Soviet Union to purchase mobile antiaircraft missiles, which the United States had been unwilling to sell Jordan, presumably because of the latter's proximity to Israel.) This is not to say that Jordan wishes to exclude the Soviets from a comprehensive settlement of the Arab-Israeli dispute. Rather, if that country wishes to participate in the establishment of peace in the area, as the king says, "it would be reasonable to give it the opportunity to participate."[21] The corollary to this is that if the Soviets are excluded they are in a position to spoil whatever progress is made. A second corollary is that the Soviets would need to contribute positively to the negotiations, e.g., by helping to influence the PLO to take positions desired by moderate Arab states.

Second, turning to Western Europe, which the king frequently visits, Jordan has developed close relationships. Many of the countries participate in Jordan's development effort, both as providers of aid and suppliers of equipment and contractors. Politically, the Western European countries have moved closer to the Jordanian and moderate Arab position with respect to the Arab-Israeli conflict. The most important and all-encompassing policy formulation was put forth at the June 1980 Venice meeting of the European Economic Community heads of government. Central to the Middle Eastern portion of the Venice Declaration was the assertion that "two principles universally accepted by the international community [are] the right to existence and to security of all the states in the region, including Israel, and justice for all the peoples, which implies the recognition of the legitimate rights of the Palestinian people." Importantly, the statement also cited the Palestinian right to self-determination and the importance of the PLO "association" with peace negotiations.[22] This declaration was obviously a consequence of European security interests, which are focused on seeking peace in the Middle East and maintaining European access to Arab oil production and markets. Additionally, it is quite apparent that it overlaps considerably with the Jordanian official position. This congruence of policy is a reflection of Jordan's articulation of the policy of the moderate Arab states and King Hussein's role as spokesman for that group of states.

NOTES

1. *Jordan Times* (Amman), quoting Prince Hassan, October 29, 1978.

2. Rami Khouri's interview with Prime Minister Sharaf, *Middle East* (London), February 1980, p. 25.

3. Ibid.

4. For an excellent discussion of legitimacy in the Arab world, see Michael C. Hudson, *Arab Politics* (New Haven, Conn.: Yale University Press, 1977).

5. *Jordan Times*, March 15, 1981, p. 1.

6. *Middle East Economic Digest* (London), February 20, 1981, p. 31.

7. *New York Times*, October 10, 1980, p. A-14.

8. Adnan Abu Odeh, "Jordan and the Middle East Crisis," *AEI Foreign Policy and Defense Review* (Washington, D.C.) 3, (1981): 12–13.

9. H.M. King Hussein Ibn Talal, "Speech Before the National Press Club," Washington, D.C., June 19, 1980, p. 7 (available from Jordan Information Bureau).

10. Abu Odeh, "Jordan and the Middle East Crisis," p. 10.

11. Ibid., p. 12.

12. Adam M. Garfinkle, "Negotiating by Proxy: Jordanian Foreign Policy and U.S. Options in the Middle East," *Orbis* 24, 4 (Winter 1981):861.

13. Ibid., pp. 865, 866-867.

14. If the Begin government were replaced by a labor coalition, the course of events in the militarily occupied territories might alter.

15. *Washington Post,* September 24, 1982, p. A31.

16. *New York Times,* May 4, 1982, p. 5.

17. Ibid.

18. "Statement Issued by the Ninth Arab Summit Conference, Baghdad, November 5, 1978," *Journal of Palestine Studies* 8, 2 (Winter 1979):204.

19. *Christian Science Monitor,* July 10, 1980, p. 1.

20. Abu Odeh, "Jordan and the Middle East Crisis"; *Newsweek,* international ed., May 23, 1981, p. 52; *Washington Post,* February 19, 1981, p. A-27; *Times* (London), April 25, 1981, p. 8.

21. *Newsweek,* international ed., May 23, 1981, p. 52.

22. Quoted in John P. Richardson, "Europe and the Arabs: A Developing Relationship," *The Link* 14, 1 (1981):11. Also see Garret Fitzgerald et al., *The Middle East and the Trilateral Countries* (New York: Trilateral Commission, 1981), pp. 23-26.

Bibliography

Abdullah, H.M. King. *My Memoirs Completed*. Translated by Harold Glidden. Washington, D.C.: American Council of Learned Societies, 1954.
_____. *Memoirs of King Abdullah of Transjordan*. New York: Philosophical Library, 1950.
Abidi, Aqil. *Jordan: A Political Study, 1948–57*. London: Asia Publishing House, 1965.
Abu Jaber, Kamel S. "The Jordanians and the People of Jordan." Manuscript to be published by the Jordanian Royal Scientific Society in 1982.
_____. "The Legislature of the Hashemite Kingdom of Jordan: A Study in Political Development." *Muslim World* 59, 3 & 4 (July–October 1969):211.
Abu Jaber, Kamel S., et al. "Socio-Economic Survey of the Badia of Northeast Jordan." University of Jordan, Amman, 1976 (mimeographed).
Abu Odeh, Adnan. "Jordan and the Middle East Crisis." *AEI Foreign Policy and Defense Review* 3, 1 (1981):8.
Antoun, Richard T. *Arab Village: A Social Structural Study of a Transjordanian Peasant Community*. Bloomington: Indiana University Press, 1972.
_____. *Low-Key Politics: Local-Level Leadership and Change in the Middle East*. Albany: State University of New York Press, 1979.
Aresvik, Oddvar. *The Agricultural Development of Jordan*. New York: Praeger Publishers, 1976.
Aruri, Naseer H. *Jordan: A Study in Political Development (1921–1965)*. The Hague: Martinus Nijhoff, 1972.
Bailey, Clinton. "Changing Attitudes Toward Jordan in the West Bank." *Middle East Journal* 32(Spring 1978):155.
Barghouti, Shawki. "The Role of Agricultural Cooperatives in Wheat Production in Jordan." Working draft, Ford Foundation, Amman, 1976.
Barhoum, Mohammed Issa. "East Jordan Valley Villagers Versus Social Institutions." University of Jordan, Amman, 1979 (mimeographed).
Al-Bukhari, Najati. *Education in Jordan*. Amman: Ministry of Information and Culture, 1972.
Central Bank of Jordan. *Monthly Statistical Bulletin*, various dates.
Dajani, Jarir S. "A Social Soundness Analysis of the Amman Water and Sewerage Systems." United States Agency for International Development, Washington, D.C., 1978 (mimeographed).

Dajani, Jarir S., and Muneera S. Murdock. "Assessing Basic Human Needs in Rural Jordan." United States Agency for International Development, Washington, D.C., 1978 (mimeographed).

Faddah, Mohammad Ibrahim. *The Middle East in Transition: A Study of Jordan's Foreign Policy.* New York: Asia Publishing House, 1974.

Fitzgerald, Garret et al. *The Middle East and the Trilateral Countries.* New York: Trilateral Commission, 1981.

Garfinkle, Adam M. "Negotiating by Proxy: Jordanian Foreign Policy and U.S. Options in the Middle East." *Orbis* 24 (Winter 1981):859.

Gibb, H.A.R. *Muhammadism.* New York: Oxford University Press, 1953.

Glubb, Sir John Bagot. *A Soldier with the Arabs.* New York: Harper & Brothers, 1957.

————. *The Story of the Arab Legion.* London: Hodder & Stoughton, 1952.

————. *Syria, Lebanon, Jordan.* New York: Walker & Company, 1967.

Goichon, A.-M. *Jordanie Reéle* [Jordan today]. Paris: G.-P. Maisonneuve and Larose. Vol. I: 1967; Vol. II: 1972.

Gotsch, Carl. "Wheat Price Policy and the Demand for Improved Technology in Jordan's Rainfed Agriculture." Discussion Paper No. 2, Ford Foundation, Amman, 1976.

Gubser, Peter. *Politics and Change in Al-Karak, Jordan.* London: Oxford University Press, 1973.

Hacker, James M. *Modern Amman.* Durham: Department of Geography, Durham Colleges, 1960.

Hill, Allen. "Population Composition, Mortality and Fertility." Unpublished paper, University of Jordan, Amman, 1977.

Howard, Norman F. "Jordan: The Price of Moderation." *Current History* 68, 402 (February 1974):62.

————. "The Uncertain Kingdom of Jordan." *Current History* 66, 390 (February 1974):62.

el-Hurani, Haitham. "Economic Analysis of the Development of the Wheat Subsector of Jordan." Ph.D. dissertation, Iowa State University, 1975.

Hyslop, John. "The Dryland Subsector of Jordanian Agriculture: A Review." United States Agency for International Development, Amman, 1976 (mimeographed).

Ibn Talal, H.M. King Hussein. *My War with Israel.* As told to and with additional material by Vick Vance and Pierre Lauer. New York: William Morrow and Co., 1969.

————. "Speech Before the National Press Club," Washington, D.C., June 19, 1980 (available from Jordan Information Bureau).

————. *Uneasy Lies the Head: The Autobiography of His Majesty King Hussein I of the Hashemite Kingdom of Jordan.* New York: Bernard Geis Associates, 1962.

International Bank for Reconstruction and Development. *The Economic Development of Jordan.* Baltimore: Johns Hopkins University Press, 1957.

Israel, Central Bureau of Statistics. *Statistical Abstract of Israel,* various years.

Jarvis, Claude Scudamore. *Arab Command: The Biography of F. G. Peake Pasha.* London: Hutchinson & Co., 1943.

Johnston, Sir Charles, *The Brink of Jordan.* London: Hamiltion, 1972.

Jordan Co-operative Organization. "The Co-operative Movement in Jordan."
    Amman, September 1979 (mimeographed).
Jordan Department of Statistics. *Agricultural Statistical Yearbook and Agricultural
    Sample Survey 1978*. Amman, 1979.
_____. *First Results of the 1979 Census*. Amman, 1980 (in Arabic).
_____. *Multi-Purpose Household Survey*. Amman, 1974.
_____. *National Accounts in Jordan, 1967–1977*. Amman, n.d. (1978?).
_____. *Statistical Yearbooks*. Amman, various years.
Jordan Ministry of Information. *Training Institutes in Jordan*. Amman, 1978.
Kanovsky, Eliyahu. *Economic Development of Jordan*. Tel Aviv: University Pub-
    lishing Projects, 1976.
Kaplan, Stephen S. "United States Aid and Regime Maintenance in Jordan,
    1957–1973." *Public Policy*, 23, 2 (Spring 1975):189–217.
Khouri, Rami G. "New Broom in Jordan." *Middle East International*, February 15,
    1980, p. 7.
Kirkbride, Sir Alec. *A Crackle of Thorns*. London: John Murray, 1956.
_____. *From the Wings: Amman Memoirs 1947–1951*. London: Frank Cass, 1976.
Kissinger, Henry. *White House Years*. Boston: Little, Brown and Co., 1979.
Kuroda, Alice K., and Yasumasa Kuroda. *Palestinians Without Palestine: A Study of
    Political Socialization Among Palestinian Youths*. Washington, D.C.: Univer-
    sity Press of America, 1978.
Lerner, Daniel. *The Passing of Traditional Society*. New York: Free Press, 1958.
Lesch, Ann M. *Political Perceptions of the Palestinians on the West Bank and the
    Gaza Strip*. Washington, D.C.: Middle East Institute, 1980.
Lutfiyya, A. M. *Baytin, a Jordanian Village*. The Hague: Mouton, 1966.
McLaurin, R. D. (ed.). *The Political Role of Minority Groups in the Middle East*.
    New York: Praeger Publishers, 1979.
al-Mady, Munib, and Sulayman Musa. *Taʾrikh al-ʾUrdun fi al-Qarn al-ʿIshrin*
    [History of Jordan in the twentieth century]. Amman?: 1959.
Majaly Hazaʾ. *Mudhakkiraty*. N.p. (Amman?), 1960.
Malkawi, Ahmad. *Regional Development in Jordan—Some Aspects of the Urban
    Bias*. Amman: Royal Scientific Society, 1978.
Maʾoz, Moshe (ed.). *Palestinian Arab Politics*. Jerusalem: Jerusalem Academic
    Press, 1975.
Mazur, Michael P. *Economic Growth and Development in Jordan*. Boulder, Colo.:
    Westview Press, 1979.
Mishal, Shaul. *West Bank/East Bank, the Palestinians in Jordan, 1949–1967*.
    New Haven, Conn.: Yale University Press, 1978.
Morris, James. *The Hashemite Kings*. New York: Pantheon, 1959.
Nyrop, Richard F., Robert Rinehart, Irving Kaplan, Darrel R. Eglin, R. S. Shinn,
    and Harold D. Nelson. *Jordan, A Country Study*. Washington, D.C.: Govern-
    ment Printing Office, 1980.
Patai, Raphael. *The Kingdom of Jordan*. Princeton, N.J.: Princeton University
    Press, 1958.
Peake, Frederick G. *History and Tribes of Jordan*. Coral Gables, Fla.: University
    of Miami Press, 1958.
al-Qasus, 'Uda. "Memoirs." Unpublished manuscript, Karak, 1920s.

Quandt, William B. *Decade of Decisions: American Policy Toward the Arab-Israeli Conflict, 1967–1976.* Berkeley: University of California Press, 1977.

Quandt, William B., Fuad Jabber, and Ann Mosely Lesch. *The Politics of Palestinian Nationalism.* Berkeley: University of California Press, 1973.

Richardson, John P. "Europe and the Arabs: A Developing Relationship." *The Link* 14 (January-March, 1981):1.

Royal Scientific Society. Various occasional economic papers, various years.

Sheehan, E.R.F. *The Arabs, Israelis, and Kissinger.* New York: Reader's Digest Press, 1976.

Shwadran, Benjamin. *Jordan: A State of Tension.* New York: Council for Middle Eastern Affairs Press, 1959.

Sinai, Ann, and Allen Pollack (eds.). *The Hashemite Kingdom of Jordan and the West Bank. A Handbook.* New York: American Academic Association for Peace in the Middle East, 1977.

"Statement Issued by the Ninth Arab Summit Conference, Baghdad, November 5, 1978." *Journal of Palestine Studies* 8 (Winter 1979):203.

Tutunji, Jenab. "Industry Favoured in New Five-Year Plan." *Middle East Economic Digest,* March 27, 1981, p. 20.

United Nations Relief and Works Agency for Palestine Refugees. *Report of the Commissioner-General of the United Nations Relief and Works Agency for Palestine Refugees in the Near East.* New York: United Nations, various years.

al-ᵓUrdun fi Khamsin ᶜAmma, 1921–1971 [Jordan during fifty years]. Amman: Ministry of Information and Culture, 1972.

Van Arkadie, Brian. *Benefits and Burdens: A Report on the West Bank and Gaza Strip Economies Since 1967.* Washington, D.C.: Carnegie Endowment for International Peace, 1977.

Vatikiotis, P. J. *Politics and the Military in Jordan: A Study of the Arab Legion, 1921–1957.* New York: Praeger Publishers, 1967.

Yacoub, Salah M. "Sedentarization and Settlement of the Nomadic Populations in Selected Countries of the ECWA Region." Paper presented at the Ninth World Congress of Sociology, August 1978 (mimeographed).

PERIODICALS

Jordan Times (Amman)
Middle East (London)
Middle East Economic Digest (London)
Middle East International (London)
Middle East Journal (Washington, D.C.)
Newsweek
New York Times
Times (London)
Washington Post

Index

135